DECADE OF DECLINE

DECADE OF DECLINE

Civil Liberties in the Thatcher Years

Peter Thornton

National Council for Civil Liberties

National Council for Civil Liberties
21 Tabard Street, London SE1 4LA

ISBN 0 946088 30 6

Acknowledgments

Thanks first and foremost to Sarah Spencer, General Secretary of NCCL, for her positive and helpful contributions. Thanks to Madeleine Colvin, Jean Coussins, Sue Dalal, Alf Dubs, Larry Grant, Paddy Hillyard, Sara Huey, Stephen Sedley QC, Chris Sallon, and Kathy Sutton, for their constructive comments on the manuscript; also to Renée Harris for her assistance. Thanks for the following contributions; Rod Robertson of NALGO on trade unions, and Kathy Sutton and Christine Jackson on women.

Thanks also for the use of much material including published information in *The Guardian, The Independent, The Times, The Observer, The Sunday Times*, in publications by the CRE, the EOC, NACRO, UKIAS, the PCA, Home Office statistics, in *The Coercive State* by Paddy Hillyard and Janie Percy-Smith (Fontana, 1988), *Bricks of Shame* by Vivien Stern (Penguin Special, 1987), *Policing by Coercion* by Louise Christian (GLC, 1983), *Shooting in the Dark* by Gerry Northam (Faber and Faber, 1988), *Immigration Law and Practice* by Lawrence Grant and Ian Martin (The Cobden Trust, 1982), and in NCCL publications, briefing papers, discussion documents, policy papers too numerous to mention.

Designed by Farrington's.
Printed by The Yale Press Limited.

1

Introduction

The last ten years of government have had a striking effect upon freedom in the United Kingdom. Civil liberties have not just been eroded; they have been deliberately attacked and undermined. The scale of the assault is breathtaking: from censorship of the media to the invasion of privacy, from increased police powers to injustice and unfairness, from a denial of basic rights to institutionalised intolerance and discrimination.

The subject of this work is the decline of freedom in the past decade. The themes are those defined by successive governments. First, the state has increased its own power at the expense of individual freedom. It has developed, for example, state censorship by banning radio and television programmes, by interfering with the right of the press to publish. It has effectively extended the laws of secrecy to deny the public's right to be informed. It has increased government control over the individual in the collection and use of personal information.

Secondly, the Government has taken away basic rights in order to stifle legitimate protest. It has diminished freedom of association and freedom of expression. Workers have been sacked for belonging to a trade union. The police have been given wide discretionary powers to ban and restrict demonstrations.

Thirdly, the Government has strengthened the powers of the servants of the state, with a corresponding reduction in the level of accountability of these servants to democratic control. The police have been given unacceptably wide powers of arrest and detention without adequate safeguards for suspects. The police are now controlled and armed by central government and autonomous chief constables. The Special Branch's responsibility is largely undefined. The security services are accountable to no one.

Fourthly, the Government has created a climate of intolerance, with institutionalised prejudice and discrimination. The immigration laws are racially discriminatory. Individual acts of racism are on the increase. Homosexuality has been attacked by Clause 28.

Travellers have been treated as outcasts.

All this has been done with the growing confidence of a long period in office. This fact alone may have serious consequences for democracy: a weakened Parliament, an acquiescent judiciary and a tamed public. But above all it has allowed the Government to become immune to rational argument. Too many people believe that the Government has stopped listening. The healthy sounds of protest and dissent are distinctly muffled.

The future is bleak. 'Bad laws', said Edmund Burke, 'are the worst sort of tyranny'. In the case of the Thatcher Governments the laws have created an undemocratic imbalance between the power of government and the rights of the individual. Many of these laws will take years to reverse. Attitudes and prejudices will take even longer. This Government, and future governments, should be reminded that 'The history of liberty is a history of limitations of governmental power, not the increase of it.' Woodrow Wilson went on to add: 'The history of liberty is a history of resistance.' We must not give up.

2

Censorship and Secrecy

Censorship and secrecy are the weapons of the authoritarian state. There is a widespread belief in this country that they are causes which the present Government happily espouses: censorship to control the free flow of information to the public; secrecy to protect the tainted decisions of the state.

The Government tried to stop the newspapers writing about *Spycatcher*. It sent the Special Branch to the BBC and the *New Statesman* to sort out the Zircon affair. It banned a perfectly harmless BBC radio programme, *My Country Right or Wrong*, without knowing what was in it. It has imposed the greatest ever peacetime controls on broadcasting.

All of these actions were put in motion by Government decision, not by the will of Parliament. As Lord Bridge, senior law lord, crisply observed in a powerful dissenting judgment in one of the many *Spycatcher* hearings, freedom of speech is always the first casualty under a totalitarian regime.

Spycatcher

Spycatcher is the memoirs of Peter Wright, a former senior MI5 agent. Wright alleges that the security services acted above the law. They committed as a matter of routine illegal acts, including the burglary and bugging of embassies, telephone tapping and mail interception without warrants. They ventured into the political arena with the investigation of left-wing groups and, in his most sensational (and subsequently according to Wright his most 'unreliable') claim, by instigating a treasonable plot to destabilise the Wilson Government.

The Government could not prosecute Wright under the Official Secrets Act. He had already retired, with a grievance about his MI5 pension, to Australia, where *Spycatcher* was first published. But distance did not stop the Government trying to stop Wright. For three years the Government pursued the suppression of *Spycatcher* in

Australia and around the world, spending over £3 million of public money. Described by one judge as 'the most litigated book of all time' and by another as 'fearfully boring', *Spycatcher* became an international bestseller. Its sales were boosted by the Government's heavy-handed attempts to ban the book in Australia and to prevent newspapers in Britain from publishing extracts or even partial summaries of Wright's allegations.

The Government claimed that Wright owed a lifelong and absolute duty of confidentiality to the Crown and that therefore he had to carry his secrets with him to the grave. Newspapers could not publish anything about the allegations in *Spycatcher*, argued the Government, because they were bound by the same duty irrespective of the circumstances under which they acquired the information.

The newspapers argued that there were wider principles at stake than the mere publication of an old man's memoirs. The secret services must operate within the law. If they were alleged to have failed to do so it was in the national interest that the press be entitled to publish the details of their alleged misdoings.

In Australia, where 'the natural fall guy' Sir Robert Armstrong, the Cabinet Secretary, admitted having been 'economical with the truth', the courts refused to ban *Spycatcher*. The Government's claim was not enforceable there; Britain could not tell the Australian courts what was in their public interest.

In Britain a series of cases against the press and a series of conflicting decisions finally ended in October 1988 with the decision in the House of Lords against the Government. The Law Lords decided that publication of *Spycatcher* abroad and the ready availability of copies in the United Kingdom had destroyed any secrecy as to its contents, so that no further damage could be done by publishing information derived from the book. The injunctions against the press were lifted.

While the final decision was welcome, however, it was not the wholesale victory that it first seemed. First, the Government had succeeded in its stated aim. It had firmly established the principle of the duty of confidentiality. That duty was not found to be absolute and unfettered by overriding public interest, as the Government had claimed, but the Government had been at least partially successful. The Law Lords condemned Wright as a traitor and were divided over the question of public interest. To this extent the Government has substantial ammunition for reform (see Chapter 3).

Secondly, this was not a judgement founded on high principle.

There was no eloquent defence of the freedom of the press or of the right of the public to receive information. On the contrary this was a pragmatic decision: the newspapers could publish because Wright's secrets were no longer secret. It was not therefore a decision which would in any way deter the Government from pursuing policies of pre-censorship of the press.

Thirdly, it was not a judgement which would force the Government to take steps to make the security services more democratically accountable. The Government has refused to set up a public inquiry into the security services. Instead, it has introduced the Security Service Bill which provides no clear role for MI5, no parliamentary accountability and no effective remedy for aggrieved individuals (see Chapter 3).

And there have been casualties along the way. In one of the *Spycatcher* hearings the Court of Appeal ruled, at the Government's request, that the law of injunctions should be extended to bind every organ of the media when one only was injuncted. In another hearing, the Law Lords extended the injunction to cover reports of the legal proceedings in Australia. This set a dangerous precedent for the freedom of the press and the public's right to information.

There are warning notes for the future, too. At one stage in the proceedings the Government suggested that the injunction banning publication of details from *Spycatcher* should extend to a permanent ban on newspapers covering 'any information concerning or arising out of the allegations made in the book *Spycatcher*', even if the press were to obtain information about the episodes in the book from other sources. This claim was rejected by the courts. So too was another Government claim for a general injunction preventing future publication of any information connected with *Spycatcher* received from any member or former member of MI5. In another hearing the Government argued (unsuccessfully) that the case should not be reported.

There were times in the three years of litigation over *Spycatcher* when the serious threat to civil liberties was masked by the more ludicrous side of events. Although still banned in Britain, *Spycatcher* has been freely available at many bookshops. Pirate copies abound and the law has not been broken by bringing copies into the country from abroad. A computer software designer who sold 490 imported copies of *Spycatcher* by the side of the A40 in west London was charged, not with selling a banned book, but with obstruction of the highway. 10,000 copies of the English translation of *Pravda*, the Russian newspaper, were impounded because they contained an article about *Spycatcher*. The Treasury Solicitor employed local solicitors to spy on respectable booksellers in different parts of the country who might have been tempted to sell copies. The High Court ruled in October 1987 that libraries could not stock the book, but extracts were read out on Danish national radio in Danish and English, on Edinburgh's *Radio Forth*, at Speakers' Corner in Hyde Park and many other places.

Nor was the Government consistent in its approach. No action was taken against *The Daily Mirror* for publishing a story which detailed one of Wright's allegations about bugging at Claridges. Nor was any attempt made by the Government to stop publication of *Spycatcher* in the USA. No doubt the Government was mindful of the inconvenient First Amendment to the American Constitution which protects freedom of expression. In the Pentagon Papers case the US Supreme Court held that the principle of freedom of expression required that no prior restraint could be placed on publication of government information, except during war time or where the lives of government agents would be put at risk.

But at least some ringing condemnations of the Government's censorship could be heard. In a letter to *The Times* Lord Scarman said that the majority of the Law Lords had overlooked the law providing the right of the public to access to information already made public: the 'fundamental law providing the right of the public to access to information already in the public domain and the public right of free speech of which the freedom of the press is an important constituent. . . Surely we need a Bill of Rights to educate all of us to our true priorities in the law.' Lord Denning was disturbed by the width of the original injunction and the introduction of prior restraint censorship.

In the *Spycatcher* hearings there were some welcome judicial observations, too. Although Lord Ackner said that to lift the injunctions would be 'a charter for traitors', Lord Bridge proclaimed that the ban amounted to 'a massive encroachment on freedom of speech'. Lord Oliver reminded us that Blackstone had observed that the liberty of the press was essential to the nature of a free state. Mr Justice Scott, in finding against the Government in one of the early hearings, said: 'The importance to the public of this country of the allegation that members of MI5 endeavoured to undermine and destroy public confidence in a democratically elected government makes the public the proper recipient of the information.' And in the final appeal, Lord Keith said: 'A government is not in a position to win the assistance of the court in restraining the publication of information imparted in confidence by it or its predecessors unless it can show that publication would be harmful to the public interest.'

The overriding impression left by the *Spycatcher* saga, however, is of a Government dedicated to increasing its control over information by censorship, a Government dedicated to extending the limits of state secrecy, and a Government prepared to force a change of the rules (as we shall see in more detail in Chapter 3) in order to avoid the scrutiny of open government.

But the Government's attention was not only focused on the press.

The Zircon affair

In January 1987 Alisdair Milne, the BBC's Director General, decided to ban a television programme about the Zircon spy satellite on grounds of national security. The programme, which had earlier been cleared by Alan Protheroe, the BBC's Assistant Director General, was one in a series of six programmes entitled *Secret Society* which had been made by the investigative journalist Duncan Campbell. The theme of the Zircon programme was that the Government had concealed the existence, and the cost (an estimated £5 million), of the Zircon satellite from Parliament in breach of an undertaking given to the Public Accounts Committee.

The ban on the programme, which was eventually shown in September 1988, led to a disturbing sequence of legal moves against Campbell, the BBC and the *New Statesman* magazine – moves which smacked of a police state mentality. The *New Statesman* employed Campbell; they decided to publish his story about Zircon and be damned. It was only then that the Government decided to act ('in the name of national security'), even though it had known of the programme as early as the summer of 1986.

The Government obtained an injunction against Campbell, and then tried to injunct Members of Parliament from viewing the programme in the House of Commons. Special Branch police officers were dispatched to raid the office of the *New Statesman* under a warrant granted to the Attorney General in a private court hearing. When asked what he thought of the film, Detective Inspector Williams in charge of the search replied: 'We're not allowed to see it. That's why this search is so difficult.' The Special Branch also searched Campbell's home at night, having broken down the door, and the homes of two other *New Statesman* journalists.

Finally, in an unprecedented move, Special Branch officers raided the Glasgow offices of BBC Scotland and seized all six films in the *Secret Society* series. Chief Inspector Stewart who led the raid warned BBC staff: 'You can do it the easy way or the hard way. If necessary we will search this building until we get what we want.' The original search warrant had been quashed by a judge for being too widely drawn. The police had to return the material they had seized until a fresh warrant was drawn up. When the police arrived the next time they realised they had brought the wrong warrant. One senior journalist present described it as 'the most frightening weekend of my life, the kind of fear I had previously associated with Eastern Europe'.

Campbell always claimed that his information was an open secret, drawn in the main from published sources including a British Aerospace press release. He further claimed that the only information which would help a foreign power was the technical information about Zircon which he never intended to publish.

The invocation of national security was seen by many as yet another use of the cloak of secrecy to conceal a cover-up. The legal moves had all the hallmarks of a campaign to intimidate the press, culminating in the knock on the journalist's door in the middle of the night. Roy Jenkins, former Home Secretary, asked the House of Commons the rhetorical question: 'What is the supreme objective for which the government are prepared to look as though they were running a second-rate police state, infused equally with illiberalism and incompetence?'

The roles of the Attorney General and the Special Branch raised concern. The Attorney General stated that he had initiated all the legal action in the Zircon affair. But the twin roles of the Attorney General – as legal guardian of the public interest and member of the Government – may conflict or appear to conflict in politically sensitive cases.

Special Branch officers occupy a unique position within the police force. Their activities are often so secret and unaccountable that local chief constables have no clear knowledge of, or control over, what they are doing. The Home Affairs Committee of the House of Commons admitted in 1984 that its inquiries into the Special Branch had been 'severely restricted' because of the 'close relations' between Special Branch and the security services. They queried why Home Office guidelines on the Special Branch had been kept secret. In the Zircon affair nobody seemed to know who was responsible for their actions and for obtaining the warrants.

But the BBC should have been warned. Threats to its independence had been clearly signalled, in this affair and elsewhere. The Zircon programme was only stopped after the intervention of Sir Peter Marychurch, head of GCHQ, the Government Communications Headquarters at Cheltenham (see Chapter 8). Even though the BBC was eventually allowed to screen the Zircon programme, another programme in the series, entitled *Cabinet*, which is about the manipulation of news by the Government, will never be shown.

It was Norman Tebbit who as Chairman of the Conservative Party (but not, he assured us, as a Government minister) crudely attacked the BBC (and the award-winning journalist Kate Adie) for its coverage of the bombing of Libya in April 1986. In 1985 the governors of the BBC had banned the *Real Lives* programme on the IRA against the wishes of the Director General.

These are only a few modern examples of external and internal censorship. There is a long list of programmes on Northern Ireland which have been banned, censored or delayed. It includes plays, documentaries, news programmes and even *Top of the Pops* in September 1981 because it contained a video by the rock group Police. *The Times* described the video as 'a collage of Ulster street scenes incorporating urchins, graffiti, Saracens and soldiers . . . it seemed good-hearted and utterly uncontentious.'

In March 1988 yet another attack came from the Government when the Prime Minister tilted at both the BBC and ITN for failing to hand over untransmitted film of the murder of two soldiers at an IRA funeral in Belfast. The broadcasting authorities defended their position by saying that to hand over such material voluntarily would be to put the camera crews at risk of serious personal violence on future assignments. The following day the Royal Ulster Constabulary, acting under the Prevention of Terrorism Act, seized all the material. Dr Colin Morris, the BBC's Northern Ireland Controller, said that faced with the possible arrest of a BBC executive he had no choice but to hand over the material.

But still more was to come.

My Country Right or Wrong

In December 1987 the Attorney General obtained another injunction to stop the broadcast of the first of three programmes in a radio series, *My Country Right or Wrong*. The programme featured interviews with three former members of MI5, with three former MI6 agents and with two ex-GCHQ employees. This action shocked the BBC. Unlike the Zircon programme which had been made by an outsider with left-wing credentials, this series was very much an internal BBC creation, a carefully muted piece of analysis. As one insider put it: 'These were not radical, challenging programmes from the wild fringes, but solid, well-researched pieces drawing on many respected political figures'. They included two former Home Secretaries, two former Defence Ministers and one former Lord Chancellor.

The Government took action after reading a diary piece in *The Daily Telegraph*. This was apparently the sole cause for concern despite a subsequent admission by the Attorney General, Sir Patrick Mayhew, that Sir Anthony Duff, the Director General of MI5, had been informed that former officers had contributed to the programme and did not object. The Treasury Solicitor, Sir John Bailey, failed to persuade the BBC to let him vet the script of the programme. So the Government went to court again, on the Prime Minister's initiative (as the Attorney General later admitted).

The injunction was obtained in a private half-hour hearing upon the now familiar basis of breach of confidence. The judge had refused a brief adjournment to allow the BBC to be represented. Only a week earlier the Government had obtained a fresh injunction against Duncan Campbell to prevent disclosure of information obtained by GCHQ employees. This injunction was later extended to order Campbell to hand over certain material. The pattern of injunctions appeared to give support to the Government's claims in the continuing *Spycatcher* hearings that there should be a blanket ban on anything relating to security.

The most sinister aspect was the scope of the wide-ranging injunction, requested by the Government and granted by the court. It banned the BBC from broadcasting any programme containing interviews with past or present members of the security and intelligence services or including information obtained from them. It also banned the identification of such individuals.

This meant that the BBC could not identify by name the very man whose allegations were at the centre of current interest in the security services. Arguably they could not report the legal proceedings concerning Wright and the press. A play about Kim Philby, the spy, had to be shelved until the injunction was lifted. It also meant that all the other organs of the media were bound by the terms of the injunction, since the Court of Appeal had ruled in a *Spycatcher* hearing that an injunction binding one part of the media bound the rest.

This time the BBC came out fighting. John Birt, the BBC's

Deputy Director General responsible for news and current affairs, described the court action as draconian: 'This is stopping us broadcasting a series of programmes which is a responsible examination of the role and accountability of the security services in a democracy. Indeed, even the secretary of the D Notice Committee [which rules on media coverage of sensitive defence issues] agreed to be interviewed only yesterday.' For his part Rear-Admiral William Higgins, the secretary of the D Notice Committee, said that he regretted the entwining of the issues of national security and the duty of confidentiality. He had welcomed the opportunity to explain in the programme the workings of the D Notice system despite being refused a request to see the script.

Less than a week later the Government agreed to modify the injunction, but only a little.

Three months later in March 1988 the Government had not surrendered its role of censorship over the series. It lifted the ban on one of the three programmes, but still prevented the other two from being broadcast.

In May 1988 the rest of the ban was lifted. The Treasury Solicitor had by then read and vetted all the scripts. Prior restraint censorship had been exercised to the full. Since then a GCHQ official has been disciplined and fined £500 for allegedly breaking security regulations including taking part in the series.

Yet another sorry chapter of state control over freedom of expression had come to an end. But there would be no softening of Government attitudes in the proposals on official secrets yet to come. Before those proposals were decided and made law, the Government imposed yet another restriction on the media.

New broadcast controls

In October 1988 the Home Secretary, Douglas Hurd, announced that broadcast interviews with terrorists in Northern Ireland and their supporters were banned. The ban was described as the first in 'a series of initiatives' against terrorism, which are likely to include the requirement to swear an oath renouncing violence for all election candidates, restrictions on defendants' right of silence and the reversal of the burden of proof in the seizure of terrorists' funds.

The ban was implemented without notice. It directs the BBC and the IBA not to broadcast interviews with members or supporters of named organisations. In particular the ban includes Sinn Fein, the political wing of the IRA, which has 56 councillors and one MP, and the Loyalist para-military Ulster Defence Association. The ban was imposed under Section 29 of the Broadcasting Act 1981 and under the BBC's charter.

There was widespread criticism of the ban. It was attacked in principle. It was a denial of free expression. It deprived the public from making its own mind up about important issues. It was a further extension of state control by censorship. It set a dangerous precedent for the control of broadcasting, and it deprived democratically elected representatives of a platform which was available to others. The ban was also attacked in practice. The wording of the directive was wide – it covers statements by people who 'support or invite support for these organisations' – and would therefore lead to difficult questions of interpretation. It was inconsistent because it did not extend to reporting of Parliament and elections. It did not ban reported speech and was therefore likely to lead to anomalies such as voice-over repetition, and to be counter-productive.

The BBC, describing the ban as 'a dangerous precedent', said that it would make Northern Ireland coverage incomplete. Lord Bonham-Carter, a former Vice Chairman of the BBC, urged the broadcasting authorities to seek judicial review of the ban. He argued that the prohibition threatened to countermand the statutory duty of the broadcasters to ensure impartiality in their output. ITN expressed the hope that the ban would not lead to further curtailment; the public was so resolutely against terrorism because reporting had been so full and free. The National Union of Journalists accused the Government of putting broadcasters under restrictions like those in South Africa. It has threatened to take the Government to the European Court of Human Rights in order to challenge the restrictions. The Bishop of Manchester said that the ban got dangerously near to eroding fundamental principles of liberty in this country, and simply handed a propaganda weapon to those whom the Government wished to fight.

The ban received such interest world-wide that President Botha of South Africa was moved to say that he would introduce similar measures. At home, the Prime Minister, Margaret Thatcher, subsequently claimed that civil liberties had to be sacrificed in the war against terrorism: 'To beat off your enemy in a war, you have to suspend some of your civil liberties for a time.'

This is the most serious restriction on broadcasting in peacetime. It marks the high point of mistrust between the Government and the media. It is the latest in a series of moves to control the free flow of information to the public, but it is unlikely to be the last.

12

3

Official Secrets:
Reform or Repression?

In pursuing the press, the media and individuals by way of injunction through the civil courts, the Government has been deliberately changing the accepted rules of censorship. Pre-*Spycatcher* there had been no prior restraint on freedom of expression. The expression 'publish and be damned' had meant exactly what it said. If a newspaper published a state secret it took the risk of prosecution – under the Official Secrets Acts.

But prosecutions have been generally unpopular, because they are brought under the discredited Section 2 of the Official Secrets Act. And in the main they have been unsuccessful, most notably in the case of Clive Ponting. The risk of failure and of unpopularity has become too great. So the Government has developed and promoted the argument of the lifelong duty of confidentiality of Crown servants and pursued the doctrine of prior restraint. For example, the radio series *My Country Right or Wrong* could go ahead providing the scripts were checked and vetted beforehand. Otherwise sweeping injunctions would be used to cancel the programmes and prevent everyone else from repeating or referring to their contents. But nobody would be prosecuted.

This policy of avoiding prosecutions by using the civil courts was seen to be on the whole more effective and reliable, from the Government's point of view. There were no juries to defend freedom of expression and to protect the liberty of the subject from oppression. Judges were inclined on the whole to accept the Government's invocation of national security. Workers at GCHQ (see Chapter 8 below) brought a legal case to challenge the fact that they were denied the right to belong to a trade union at their place of work. In finding against them the House of Lords upheld the Government's claim for the overriding consideration of national security. Once the Government had produced some evidence to substantiate their claim that the denial of a fundamental right was based on grounds of national security, the courts could not inquire further.

But the policy had been applied inconsistently, because the Government had so far been applying it on a case by case basis.

Mr Justice Scott had remarked upon this inconsistency in one of the *Spycatcher* hearings. In March 1981 the Government took no action when Chapman Pincher's book *Their Trade is Treachery* was published. The central theme of his book was that Sir Roger Hollis, former head of MI5, had been suspected of being a Soviet spy. This was based on conversations he had with Peter Wright. It was a theme which recurred in *Spycatcher*.

On the other hand, post-*Spycatcher*, the Government did try and suppress extracts from the memoirs of Anthony Cavendish, a former MI6 officer, which were published in Scottish newspapers. Cavendish published his memoirs himself and sent them round to friends in Christmas cards. Entitled *Inside Intelligence* they set out to defend the reputation of his friend, Sir Maurice Oldfield, disputing that he had had homosexual relations with young men while he was Ulster security chief. Nevertheless the Scottish Courts provided another set-back for the Government. They dismissed the Government's case on the basis that the information was already in the public domain and because there was no justification for tilting the balance against freedom of speech and information. Nevertheless, the Government stopped distribution of the December 1988 issue of the American magazine *Harper's* because it contained extracts from Cavendish's book. The publisher of *Harper's,* John MacArthur, said: 'This is not about top secret information. It is about government control of information. It is about government tyranny and authoritarianism.'

Cavendish complained that the Government had changed the ground rules. He said that the question of lifelong silence was 'a red herring' and one which did not exist during his time in the service. Cavendish has since urged the Government to set up a proper system for vetting manuscripts of former members of the security and intelligence services, such as the CIA operates in the USA, in order to avoid falling foul of the 'bloody-mindedness of the bureaucrats who run the intelligence services'.

By contrast no restriction was placed on the publication in June 1988 of *The Friends – Britain's Post-War Intelligence Operations* by Conservative MP Rupert Allason (under the nom de plume Nigel West), even though his book contains material provided by intelligence officers and details of some of the operations that also appear in *Spycatcher*. Nor was any restriction placed on the publication in May 1988 of *The Secret Servant*, a biography of the former MI6

Director-General, Sir Stewart Menzies, by Anthony Cave Brown, even though it contains interviews with former intelligence officers.

If the Government's policy was inconsistent, it was also incomplete. In the Government's view it needed amplification and refinement. Above all it needed a new statutory framework which would also do away with Section 2 of the Official Secrets Act. In 1988 the Government therefore brought forward a White Paper with proposals for reform followed by the Official Secrets Bill and the Security Service Bill (see below).

The Official Secrets Acts

The Official Secrets Acts 1911-1939 have long been criticised, but never repealed. Section 1 of the Official Secrets Act 1911, the principal Act, is used in cases of spying. But although Section 1 provides a maximum sentence of 14 years for serious breaches of national security – George Blake, the Russian spy, was sentenced to 42 years by virtue of consecutive sentences – it is not limited to spying. It has also been used to convict members of the Committee of 100, a group of anti-nuclear protestors, who held a demonstration at Wethersfield Airfield, a prohibited place.

Section 2 of the Official Secrets Act 1911 provides for sentences of up to two years for the 'wrongful communication etc of information'. Described by the Franks Committee in 1972 as a catch-all section and 'a mess', Section 2 is 41 lines long. It embraces a wide range of activity, including the possession, retention, or communication of secret documents or information obtained by or from a Crown servant contrary to the safety or interests of the state. 'It catches', said Franks, 'all official documents and information. It makes no distinction of kind, and no distinction of degree . . . A blanket is thrown over everything; nothing escapes'.

Section 2 has frequently been used where information has been leaked to the press, often without security implications. The Section does not use the expression 'national security'; it uses the broader wording of 'the interests of the state'. In the Ponting case the Government argued – and the trial judge, Mr Justice McCowan, ruled – that the limits of 'the interests of the state' should be decided by the government of the day. Clive Ponting, a senior Whitehall civil servant, had leaked to a Member of Parliament two documents about events in the Falklands war which led up to the sinking of the Argentine cruiser *General Belgrano* in May 1982. In effect he had alleged a political cover-up.

Ponting's defence at his trial at the Old Bailey was that the public had the right to know, and that the communication to an MP (which was passed on to a Select Committee of the House of Commons) was in 'the interests of the state'. Despite the judge's ruling the jury found Ponting not guilty. Sarah Tisdall, a clerk in the private office of the Foreign Secretary, had not been so lucky. Her conscience brought her a sentence of six months imprisonment. In 1983 she sent copies of Ministry of Defence minutes on the arrangements for the arrival of US cruise missiles at the RAF base at Greenham Common to the press. On advice she pleaded guilty to a Section 2 offence. In neither case had the Government alleged that national security was involved.

In 1977 an ex-soldier and two journalists were prosecuted for giving and receiving information about signals operations. The charges were brought by the Labour Government despite its announcement shortly beforehand that Section 2 would be reformed so as to make the receipt of information of this kind no longer a criminal offence. The case was known as the ABC trial after the initials of the defendants Crispin Aubrey, John Berry and Duncan Campbell. All three were convicted. The former soldier received a suspended sentence and the two journalists were given the lightest possible sentences, conditional discharges.

Members of the Conservative Party have also fallen foul of Section 2. In 1939 the Conservative MP Duncan Sandys was warned that he risked prosecution for failing to name the person who gave him information which he had used as the basis for a Parliamentary Question about London's anti-aircraft defences. In 1971 Jonathan Aitken, now a Conservative MP, was prosecuted with the editor of the *Sunday Telegraph* for an article which he wrote on British military aid to the Nigerian Government during the Biafra war. They were both acquitted. Mr Justice Caulfield had warned in his summing-up that Section 2 'in its present form could be viciously or capriciously used by an embarrassed executive'.

The repeal of the Official Secrets Act, an Act which was passed by Parliament in forty minutes during a time of emergency, is long overdue. As Lord Scarman has said: 'I would like to see the Official Secrets Act repealed lock, stock and barrel and replaced by a much more narrowly defined protective measure and by a Freedom of Information Act.' The Government has other ideas.

The Government's proposals in the White Paper and the Official Secrets Bill are characterised by the following unwelcome features: a presumption of secrecy in favour of the Government; no provision for freedom of information (the disclosure of information will be determined by ministers); absolute criminal offences for certain categories of information disclosed; no public interest defence; no defence that the information was already in the public domain; and no parliamentary scrutiny of the security and intelligence services (see the Security Service Bill, below).

Categories   The Official Secrets Bill sets out six categories of unauthorised disclosure of official information which would be subject to prosecution under the criminal law. The six cateogries are security and intelligence, defence, international relations, information obtained in confidence from foreign governments and international organisations, information useful to criminals, and interception of communications. The maximum penalty for disclosing information in these categories would be two years' imprisonment.

In the key category of security the Government has drawn the cloak of secrecy more tightly around the operations of the security and intelligence services. Absolute offences (offences which are committed whatever the person's intention or motive) are created for primary disclosers and leakers. The disclosure of any information by serving or former members of the security and intelligence services would be an absolute offence. Disclosure of information about the activities of GCHQ, for example, by members of the security forces, however unlawful those activities, would be an absolute offence.

This category, which imposes absolute silence, is a flexible category. It can be extended to 'designated' persons, for example, to police officers (say John Stalker or members of the Special Branch), who become involved in sensitive areas.

For journalists and other secondary disclosers who repeat the allegations, guilt would be proved where a broad test of harm were satisfied. The prosecution would have to show that the disclosure was likely to damage the operation of the security or intelligence services. But ministers have already admitted that journalists could be placed in the same position as primary disclosers and therefore no test of harm would have to be proved. This would be done by making journalists legal accessories to those bound to absolute silence and therefore as guilty as the primary disclosers.

In some categories, like defence and international relations, a test of harm would have to be satisfied, although the test is different for each category. For defence, for example, the prosecution would have to prove that the disclosure was likely either to prejudice the capability of the armed forces to carry out any of their defence tasks, or to lead to a risk of loss of life, injury to personnel or damage to equipment or installations, or to prejudice dealings between the Government and the government of another state or an international organisation.

But in some categories there is no test of harm and any unauthorised disclosure is considered to be harmful. In the interception of communications category, for example, it would be an absolute offence to reveal from official sources the name of a person whose telephone had been tapped or whose mail had been intercepted even though the tap or intercept had been made unlawfully without the necessary warrant. This would include the disclosures by the former MI5 agent Cathy Massiter of illegal tapping (see below and Chapter 4). Other categories of disclosure would be dealt with by internal civil service procedures. The White Paper implies that the Civil Service Discipline Code will have to be extended to take account of the new provisions. Also ministers are considering amending the 'conduct rules for Crown servants' by imposing a new copyright law on civil servants to prevent leaks not covered by the reforms. In effect this would prohibit civil servants from publishing anything without Government permission. Penalties for default could include dismissal, fines on pensions and seizure of profits of publications.

Defences   The most worrying aspect of the White Paper's proposals is that there is no recommendation for a general defence of disclosure in the public interest. Such a defence did exist under the original Official Secrets Act of 1889 and in a modified form under the 1911 Act, but the White Paper asserts that the need for it is outweighed by the need for clarity in the law and the need for protection of information. It would be no defence that the disclosure exposed that Parliament was misled, or that maladministration had occurred or that fraud or negligence had occurred, or that the security services had acted illegally. Nor would it be a defence that the information was already in the public domain (as with many of Peter Wright's allegations).

Critics   The Official Secrets Bill has been widely criticised for

18

widening the net of the control of information and for denying the public legitimate access to government information. It will make it easier for officials, journalists and newspapers to be prosecuted successfully for disclosing information about the operation of government and the activities of its servants.

The Press Council has warned that the proposals could make newspapers little more than government propaganda agents. The Campaign for Freedom of Information believes that the lack of a public interest defence is contrary to the existing common law.

Previous Bills   A Private Member's Bill, the Official Information Bill, proposed by Conservative MP Richard Shepherd was defeated when the White Paper was announced. If it had become law it would have provided three lines of defence: that the disclosure of official information was in the public interest; that the disclosure was not likely to harm the interests of the nation; or that the contents of the disclosure had already appeared elsewhere. Shepherd has also said that prosecutions should be brought only when the prosecution could prove that disclosure would be likely to lead to serious injury to the public interest, a test which would not have permitted the prosecution of Tisdall or Ponting. In both of those cases the Government conceded that national security was not involved.

Shepherd's Bill was a modified version of the heavily criticised 1979 Protection of Information Bill, a Bill which did not survive when it was realised that it would have allowed the prosecution of newspapers for making disclosures about Anthony Blunt, the self-confessed Soviet agent. It was also the Bill which provided the infamous proposal that a minister alone could decide what information was secret. Labour governments had promised twice to repeal Section 2, in 1974 and again in 1976, but failed to do so.

The safeguards of the Shepherd Bill are largely missing from the Government's proposals, which Shepherd described as 'a very repressive measure indeed . . . It is illiberal and it is not consonant with the experience and practice of Canada, Australia or the United States.

Freedom of information   There is a very real absence here of any semblance of a freedom of information proposal as part of the package. The public need information so that they can judge the government of the day and call it to account. The White Paper side stepped the issue by stating that the question of public access to official information 'does not arise directly out of the reform of

Section 2'.

In short the Government has put forward a carefully modulated deal which amounts to more secrecy and less information. If the White Paper seemed at first to be a little more modest than expected, it was only because engineered leaks of severe powers, such as the removal of trial by jury in official secrets cases, had paved the way for sighs of relief. In a national opinion poll 65% of those polled were in favour of a Freedom of Information Act. As Shepherd has said: 'Secret government doesn't necessarily mean better government. There is a good case for saying it means worse government.'

The Security Service Bill

In December 1988 the Government introduced the Security Service Bill. It places MI5, the Security Service, on a statutory footing for the first time. The intention behind the Bill is to head off further defeats before the European Court of Human Rights. In the Hewitt and Harman case (see Chapter 4) the European Commission has already ruled that the Government must answer the allegation that the two women were classified as subversive by MI5 while working for NCCL. In another case a financial analyst was secretly vetted and refused a job with a private company involved with Government defence contracts. The Government has indicated that it will use the Security Service Bill as a means of enforcing a 'friendly settlement' in these cases. It is an irony that the former case only came to light as a result of the 'whistle-blowing' of Cathy Massiter, a former MI5 agent. Under the new Official Secrets Act, which allows for no public interest defence, whistle-blowing of this kind will be illegal.

The Security Service Bill replaces the 1952 Maxwell Fyfe Directive and extends the remit of MI5 to 'the protection of national security', a concept undefined in the Bill. It specifically legalises bugging, burglary and telephone tapping by the security services. It adopts the wide definition of 'subversive' which is already used for civil service vetting (see Chapter 4) and which is so wide that it includes perfectly lawful, non-violent political activity.

At the same time the Bill fails to provide any adequate control of MI5, a service costing £100 million a year, by Parliament or any other independent body, as in the USA, Canada, Australia and much of Europe. Instead it perpetuates the supervision of the services by ministers, a system which has been proved to be ineffective.

The Bill also borrows features of window-dressing from the Interception of Communications Act 1985 (see Chapter 4); a Commissioner to monitor warrants and a tribunal to receive complaints from the public. Neither is likely to provide 'an effective remedy' to an aggrieved person as guaranteed by Article 13 of the European Convention of Human Rights.

Far from being 'an essay in openness' as Douglas Hurd, the Home Secretary, has claimed, the combined effect of the Security Service Bill and the Official Secrets Bill is to give the Government greater powers to withhold and conceal information. A Bill, such as the Security Service Bill, that provides no clear role for MI5, no Parliamentary accountability and no effective remedy for aggrieved individuals cannot be said to be a serious attempt to tackle the problem of safeguarding the rights of individuals as required by Europe.

4

Privacy and Confidentiality

If public life should be open and public, private life should be closed and private. State invasion of privacy should be reduced to a minimum, and confidential personal information should be kept confidential.

Contrary to these basic principles successive governments have caused and condoned the increased control over things private, notably in the collection and storage of personal and private information, but without providing the necessary safeguards to protect the liberty of the individual.

Unlike many other countries we have no Privacy Act to protect us from the invasion of privacy and personal harassment, whether by the state or by the media or other organisation. There is precious little in the law to prevent illegal telephone tapping, bugging or any other unlawful means of surveillance. The changes which have been made – in the Data Protection Act 1984, in the Consumer Credit Act 1974, and in the Interception of Communications Act 1985 – are token protection for the individual compared with the solid statutory protection which some other countries provide.

Telephone tapping, bugging and other surveillance techniques

The incidence of state surveillance over individuals will always be greater than the state admits. State surveillance 'in the interests of the state' is always likely to be unnecessarily wide. The extent of the surveillance is, of course, secret, although in October 1988 *The Observer* claimed that a huge increase in the frequency and number of official telephone taps had occurred in the last decade without the knowledge or consent of Parliament. The report claimed that the number of British Telecom tapping engineers had increased by 50% in the last eight years and that they now deal with an estimated 30,000 taps a year at a cost of £10 million.

Occasional glimpses into the operations of the security services and the Special Branch (see Chapter 2) give good cause for arguing that state surveillance is massively excessive and routinely out of lawful control.

In 1985 Cathy Massiter and another MI5 agent (who wished to remain anonymous) revealed on television that NCCL, trade unions and the peace movement were considered subversive and therefore subject to routine surveillance by the Special Branch and the security services. Certain individuals within these organisations had been targeted because they were then, or had been before, members of the Communist Party. It was further alleged that the Defence Secretary, Michael Heseltine, had had CND members' telephones tapped. Before resigning from the service Massiter had complained to senior civil servants that she considered the surveillance to be in breach of internal guidelines. She was told to see a psychiatrist.

Legal action to remedy these wrongs has yet to be successful. CND complained first to the new independent tribunal set up under the Interception of Communications Act (see below). No reasons were given for turning down the complaint. CND then complained to the High Court about the misuse of state power for political purposes. They claimed that the Home Secretary, Leon Brittan, had authorised a warrant to tap their telephones and the information had been used by Heseltine to attack CND during the 1983 general election campaign. The Court refused to intervene. Some redress, however, may be found in Europe. In June 1988 the European Commission of Human Rights found in an interim decision that the Government had a case to answer on allegations that two former officers of NCCL, Patricia Hewitt and Harriet Harman, had been placed under surveillance by MI5 (see Chapter 3).

Modern technology will no doubt improve surveillance techniques and make them more difficult to detect. In the magazine *New Statesman and Society* the journalist Duncan Campbell has alleged that the Government, in collaboration with the USA, is involved in a secret plan to expand the capacity of two electronic spy bases in Britain to eavesdrop on domestic telephone calls. Campbell claims that the plan is part of a multi-million dollar programme by the United States to modernise worldwide satellite eavesdropping. The Foreign Office and the Ministry of Defence have refused to comment on the story.

Interception of Communications Act

There is no reason to believe that the Interception of Communications Act 1985 will have any real impact on illegal surveillance. If

24

anything, the Act has a merely cosmetic function, designed to give the impression that the Government has done something, having been forced to act by the decision of the European Court of Human Rights in the Malone case in 1984. The Government was criticised by the Court for its lack of legal controls on telephone tapping.

The Act regularises the previous practice of obtaining a warrant not from a court but from the Home Secretary before interception can take place. The Home Secretary must be satisfied under one of three extremely broad heads before he grants a warrant; that the warrant is in the interests of national security; that it is required for the purpose of preventing or detecting serious crime; or that it is required for the purpose of safeguarding the economic well-being of the UK. Any unauthorised interception is a criminal offence punishable with up to two years imprisonment.

But the Act contains a number of weaknesses. It fails to cover bugging and surveillance devices, despite a clear recommendation by the Younger Committee on privacy in 1972. It fails to allow for prior judicial warrant before telephone taps are authorised, despite the recommendation of the Royal Commission on Criminal Procedure in 1981. It does not allow scrutiny in court of illegal telephone tapping. There are no safeguards to prevent interception of confidential conversations, such as those between doctor and patient or social worker and client, or of communications covered by legal professional privilege such as between lawyer and client. One warrant can cover a whole organisation, and therefore permit the invasion of privacy of thousands of people.

The Act purports to provide an additional safeguard for the aggrieved individual, by an appeal to a tribunal established under the Act to investigate complaints. But the tribunal has narrow terms of reference. It can only investigate where a warrant is already in existence; it has no power to investigate illegal interceptions. At best this system will catch the incautious police officer who sells information to an outsider. But it is unlikely to catch routine wrongdoing by insiders, whether for political or other purposes.

At the end of an investigation by the tribunal, the individual will have no right to be informed that his or her telephone has been tapped. Nor does the Act provide any remedy in the civil courts for unauthorised tapping, bugging or interception by post. In the last eight months of 1987 the Intercept Tribunal received thirty-two complaints from members of the public. No contraventions of the Act were found.

Furthermore the Act does not cover 'automatic call tracing', which, according to the authors of *Stranger on the Line – The Secret History of Phone Tapping*, is a digital computer tap within System X, the computer-run telephone system. Developed by Plessey, which has had close links with GCHQ, this system is said to leave no physical presence and is therefore beyond the reaches of the Act. The book, by Patrick Fitzgerald and Mark Leopold, also claims that GCHQ advised the police on telephone tapping during the miners' strike of 1984-85.

Police National Computer (PNC)

The scope of the information kept in police computers is extremely wide. The PNC has two main sorts of information: details of the registration of motor vehicles and details of the criminal records, including spent convictions, of more than four million individuals. It also stores information on wanted and missing persons, holds a fingerprint index and provides limited crime pattern analysis.

But the most sinister aspect of information collection is the storage of information about people who are not known criminals or even suspected of being criminals. This information is usually gathered at a local level and passed in each police station to a specially designated operator, known as the 'collator'. Much of this information is stored on local police computers. The Manchester police computer has a capacity for holding records on 300,000 people. It has been designed to make information available to patrolling officers in seconds, but with no claims as to the accuracy or reliability of the information disclosed. In one criminal case in which the prosecution disclosed to the defence that the jury would be vetted, the local information included political activities of potential jurors as well as information that one lived in a 'squat'.

The PNC is now overloaded and will soon be replaced, it is reported, by a new master computer with increased capacity for intelligence information.

Meanwhile information on the PNC is not hard to come by. A private detective can apparently gain access to information without much difficulty. It requires the co-operation of a serving police officer or administrative officer who has access to the PNC and may be paid for the information provided. Most private eyes are either 'ex-job' (former serving police officers) or have good working relationships with serving officers. Sometimes the collator will help.

In one case a serving Essex police officer was himself working in and out of hours as a private detective and using his easy access to the

PNC to trace vehicles and check job references. He also used his expertise in police surveillance to make telephone interceptions in divorce cases. He only got caught because he made a PNC vehicle check on a car which had been following an associate. It happened to be a security services vehicle, and all checks on such vehicles are run back through the system to be checked by the security services.

Blacklisting

Except where it is held on computers (see below) the storage and use of most personal information by private and public agencies continues unchecked by legislation. In most cases the information is collected without the knowledge, and certainly without the consent, of the person concerned. It may be inaccurate or out of date.

The Economic League   One private organisation, the Economic League, provides a blacklisting service to more than 2,000 British firms. It keeps secret files on allegedly subversive workers, alleging links with left-wing political groups or radical causes such as CND or feminism, or trade union activity such as taking part in a strike or sit-in. This information is obtained from subscribing companies, newspaper cuttings and other sources of information including paid informers.

Richard Brett, a former regional director of the Economic League, has said that the League's security was poor and its records unreliable. He said it was wrong that a self-appointed and publicly unaccountable group should be able to influence the job prospects of thousands of people. A Granada World in Action television programme in February 1987 demonstrated that people on the blacklist could be deprived of employment; that some of the information was inaccurate; and alleged that some of the information came from police sources. A complaint by the Economic League that the programme was unjust and unfair was later rejected by the Broadcasting Complaints Commission.

MI5 blacklisting   Isobel Hilton, a journalist, was a casualty of MI5 blacklisting. She was prevented from joining the BBC because she was on a secret list. Her case was taken up by NCCL, but the European Commission of Human Rights ruled against her in October 1988. The Commission found that she could not provide incontrovertible proof that she had suffered any loss, because she had obtained a job with the *Daily Express*.

MI5 did admit that it had secretly vetted Hilton in 1977 and had advised the BBC, without her knowledge, that she should be blacklisted. MI5 said that, as a student, she had been secretary of the Scotland-China Association which was regarded as subversive, despite having eminent churchmen, academics and a former governor of Stirling Castle among its members. But by 1977 Hilton had resigned from the Association.

In September 1987 it was reported that MI5 tried to have Anna Ford, the broadcaster, blacklisted from the BBC in the mid-1970s on the grounds that a former boyfriend had once been a communist. It is believed that in that period local Special Branch officers recruited journalists in the BBC and ITV companies to pass on information about colleagues.

In September 1988 it was alleged that Jack Dromey, a senior trade union official and former chairman of NCCL, had also been blacklisted by MI5 because of his involvement with the Grunwick strike in the late 1970s and his links with NCCL. This allegation is made in *Blacklist* by Mark Hollingsworth and Richard Norton-Taylor.

The authors also claim that former trade union leaders Jack Jones and Hugh Scanlon were listed as 'subversive' between 1966 and 1977. Scanlon, now Lord Scanlon, was prevented from becoming chairman of British Shipbuilding because MI5 advised that he should not see documents marked Confidential or above. Jones, who was made a Companion of Honour in 1978 and is now a leading campaigner for pensioners, says: 'I think the whole business is outrageous, the most worrying feature is that statements and reports are made without the knowledge of the people concerned and there are no means to question or seek redress.'

Civil service vetting   The civil service operates its own system of blacklisting. In April 1985 the Prime Minister announced revised security procedures for all 'public servants'. This category includes British Telecom and private companies engaged on Ministry of Defence work. The procedures amplify the old definition of 'subversive' to include persons who belong to an organisation 'whose aims are to *undermine* or overthrow Parliamentary democracy in the United Kingdom of Great Britain and Northern Ireland by *political, industrial* or violent means' (author's emphasis).

This wholly subjective test is applied without any right of appeal by the head of each Government department. He will decide whether membership of a particular organisation falls foul of the 'subversive' test. If it does, the applicant for a post in the department will be turned down without being told the reason. The test may also be applied inconsistently. The head of one department may come to a different conclusion to that of another department. Membership of CND could be considered subversive in the Ministry of Defence but not in the Department of Health and Social Security.

The poll tax

The proposed poll tax, or 'community charge' as it is known in the Local Government Finance Act, will pose serious threats to the privacy of the entire adult population in the way it is likely to be administered and enforced. By creating local registers of all adults and enabling their movements to be monitored, it will also provide the potential for greater control by the state over the individual.

The Government intends that, in order to prevent people evading the poll tax, poll tax staff should have the power to search through existing records which contain personal information provided for an entirely different purpose. These records will include the electoral register, lists of local library users and lists of council house tenants. The Government has denied that sensitive information within education, housing and social services records will be touched, but it insists that the names and addresses of all those using those services should be available. These records are already being used in preparation for the arrival of the poll tax.

Private agencies will also be involved in the passing of information. British Telecom is putting up £4 million in conjunction with Capita, an information technology consultancy, to create Information Exchange. This will be a national poll tax computer to help track people's movements around the country and chase unpaid community charge bills, another step along the path to requiring everybody to carry identity cards (see below).

Local government officers will be required to decide whether people sharing a house are living together as man and wife and are therefore liable for each other's tax or whether they are separated. Unpublished guidelines refer to the recovery of unpaid tax from a deserted wife by forcing her to pay her husband's share, even by seizing her chattels or attaching her earnings. The officers will have to discover the facts by whatever means are available, including intrusive questioning and, as the Borough Treasurer in Hove has suggested, the use of anonymous information and access to details in

DHSS files.

The administration of the poll tax is based on the premise that local authorities can transfer personal information given to them for entirely different purposes to the poll tax staff. The individual has the right to see their entry on the poll tax register, but a second secret manual file can be kept to which access will be denied. The Data Protection Registrar has warned the Government that there is an inherent conflict between the effectiveness of a community charge system and the privacy of individuals.

Tax evasion cannot be condoned, but the social consequences in transferring personal information without the individual's consent are serious and make this method of tax collection undesirable. The penalty for non-payment could be greater than the financial loss. In a child abuse case, for example, the mother of a child might be reluctant to give the full picture about members of the household and visitors to the house if she knew that they had not paid their poll tax.

Identity cards

At present the Government claims that it has no firm intention of introducing identity cards. But the Home Secretary has confirmed (in July 1988) that he has asked the police to make an 'updated and considered assessment' of the case for a compulsory system of national identity cards. The Government does support specific identity documents to cover, for example, football grounds and public houses.

Britain has not had national identity cards since 1952 when the system set up in the 1939-45 war was finally laid to rest. For many years the police have not favoured identity cards, but in early 1988 the Metropolitan Police Commissioner, Sir Peter Imbert, predicted that the European changes of 1992 would bring a change in the law requiring every citizen to carry an identity card. He argued that this change would contribute to the fight against crime, but felt that the system should be operated by the DHSS or the Post Office as the police did not have enough manpower to enforce it.

The civil liberty issues raised by identity cards are considerable. An individual identity card with each person having a unique PIN or personal number could lead to access to a wide range of data bases. It could list people's criminal convictions, provide confidential medical and social work records or DHSS information, and give details of employment history. There is no limit to its uses. It would provide the excuse for the establishment of the first national data base on the population, giving a number of agencies access to personal information. The card holder might have no means of checking the accuracy of the information, particularly if the card were computer readable.

Access to the card could also be given to banks, as in some European countries where the identity card is used as a bank card, and to retailers, and local authorities for poll tax enforcement (as Conservative MP Ian Bruce has argued). The poll tax will certainly mean that every adult's identity and movements could be marked out and traced.

The other civil liberty issue is enforcement. The scheme would have to be mandatory to work. Before the war-time card was abolished, Lord Chief Justice Goddard, in a case involving a motorist's refusal to show his identity card to a policeman, remarked: 'Because the police may have powers it does not follow that they ought to exercise them on all occasions or as a matter of routine . . . such action tends to make the people resentful of the acts of the police, and incline them to obstruct the police instead of assisting them.' In Germany fines can be awarded on the spot for failing to carry the card. In Belgium, Luxemburg, Spain and Portugal failure to show a card can lead to administrative detention.

The stop and search powers in Britain could be extended to cover proof of identity at any time and any place. Some senior police officers have expressed fears that card checks on black youths would lead to conflict and resentment. Others believe that a black market for fake identity cards for criminals would develop and prosper. In France the police have been accused of harassing young people and black people by demanding to see cards, for example on the Metro, on the pretext of suspected crime. In West Germany the police have checked trains and buses travelling to demonstrations and noted the identity number of people on them.

The Government may try out other schemes for identity cards first before moving on to a national scheme. A national football club membership scheme, with up to five and a half million names on a central computer, will be in force by the spring of 1990. It will be a criminal offence to give false information to obtain a card. All 16 year olds are now issued with machine readable national insurance cards and passports when they apply.

The United States, Canada and Japan have no national system of identity cards. In Australia the Government tried to introduce one in 1986 and again in 1987, but failed in the face of intense public opposition. In Western Europe there are universal systems in some countries but not in others. Where systems do exist there are wide variations in the strictness with which they are applied.

In this country we pride ourselves in the freedom to walk down the street or to stay at home without unnecessary requests from officials for identification. The onus should therefore rest on those who propose a scheme to prove that it would benefit society as a whole. There is scant evidence that identity cards help to prevent crime or catch offenders. There is much evidence from other countries that it is inconvenient, unnecessary and an invasion of privacy.

Data protection

The fears about data storage are a growing modern concern. These fears are echoed in statute form in the Data Protection Act of 1984. The Act allows every adult and every child the right to see personal records held on computer.

But the Act is inadequate. It does not extend to manual files at all. The right of access to many personal files on computer is confusing and in some cases limited. There is a right of access under the Act to medical and social work files held on a computer, but there are two major exemptions. Data may be withheld if it is likely either to cause harm to the health of the individual or to lead to the identification of a third person (not professionally involved) who has not consented to such disclosure. Education records have no such exemptions.

The Act also excludes information stored for national security reasons. The Data Protection Registrar has been given no power to issue enforcement notices to the security services and no powers of entry and inspection.

Furthermore transfers of data by a registered data user, such as a hospital or any government department or local authority, to an unregistered user, such as the security services and the Special Branch, are not shown on the public register. To make matters worse 'national security' is defined under the Act as being whatever the relevant minister says it is (see the Ponting case in Chapter 3).

Serious mistakes can be made without any form of redress. In March 1981 Jan Martin applied for a job assisting former BBC broadcaster Michael Barrett in the production of industrial films. Barrett was told by one of his clients, Taylor Woodrow, that she 'would not be welcome' on their premises because she had a connection 'with terrorists in Europe'. Martin had the good fortune to have a father who was a senior police officer at Scotland Yard. He found out that the information had been leaked by the Special Branch. Martin and her husband had stopped at a cafe while on holiday in Holland. The proprietor thought that her husband looked like a Baader-Meinhof terrorist and called the police. The Dutch police realised an innocent mistake had been made and did not even interview the couple. But the information was picked up by Special Branch and passed on.

The Act also excludes in part information stored for crime detection and taxation purposes, and in 1987 the exemption categories were extended by the Government to cover information held by financial regulatory bodies on their members, and adoption records and records about special educational needs.

Furthermore every check on an entry costs up to £10 and may take up to 40 days to complete. Following a survey, the Freedom of Information Campaign reported in November 1988 that many people were deterred from applying to see their records by the cost. Because people are charged extra to see personal information held for different purposes, the cost of applying to a single organisation can be as much as £50 or more. The report also found that some institutions did not keep to the 40 day limit.

Data can only be traced through the Data Protection Registrar if organisations register. By the end of 1987 an estimated 100,000 organisations had failed to do so. By mid-1988 the number was still approximately 80,000 and only one firm had been prosecuted for non-registration. The official deadline was May 1986.

The Act makes it an offence for a computer user to hold personal details about others without first notifying the Registrar. But the Registrar, with very limited staff resources, has been reluctant to use his powers to seize material and bring prosecutions.

Access to manual records

The Government has taken no steps to extend data protection to manual files. Most information held other than in a computer, for example in a card index or filing cabinet, falls outside the scope of the Data Protection Act. A number of Western European states include manual records in their legislation. The majority of complaints in those countries are about manual records. In the USA, the Privacy Act makes no distinction between computerised and manual records. In this country a vast number of organisations are beyond the law by keeping to manual systems.

In the face of Government inactivity a number of backbench MPs have tried to extend the scope of the law, with some modest success. The Liberal MP Archy Kirkwood, sponsored by the Freedom of Information Campaign, made some inroads with two Private Members Bills which became the Access to Personal Files Act 1987 and the Access to Medical Reports Act 1988.

The 1987 Act enables the Minister to make regulations for access to local authority housing and social services records. In early 1989 there will be a right of access to social work files held manually, although with broadly similar exceptions as those used to restrict access to computer files. There is also a Government undertaking to extend the Act to education records in 1989. The 1988 Act, however, was passed in a form so modified by Government opposition that it has limited effect. It allows people to inspect their medical records before they are sent to employers or insurers, although exemption clauses permit doctors to refuse the information on the grounds that disclosure would be likely to harm an individual's physical or mental health or if it would reveal information about a third party. Otherwise there is still no right of access to medical files held manually.

Another Private Member's Bill, which became the Local Government (Access to Information) Act 1985, requires local authority sub-committees to make available for inspection all agenda reports, minutes of meetings and background papers.

Meanwhile in Australia greater openness has led to a better understanding between Government agencies and individuals. The Freedom of Information Act of 1982 led to the public availability of internal policy and procedure manuals of departments, including the department responsible for immigration policy. The publication of 'hidden law' has improved the quality of decision making and the public's understanding of it, according to a senior Home Office official who has been studying the operation of freedom of information laws in different parts of the world.

5

Police Powers

In recent years the Government has pursued a deliberate policy of increasing police powers over the citizen. The Public Order Act, the Prevention of Terrorism Act, the Emergency Powers Act in Northern Ireland, and the Police and Criminal Evidence Act all contain a harsh, and sometimes draconian, regime of control over the individual. Between them these statutes reduce the right of legitimate protest, authorise detention and arrest without charge for up to seven days, perpetuate internal exile without trial, continue to allow for internment and non-jury courts in Northern Ireland, and devise an austere scheme for police powers of stop and search, arrest and detention.

The Public Order Act

The right of protest in public by march and meeting, vigil and picket, is an essential element of our democratic process. There is no statutory right of assembly and there never has been, but this basic right has been recognised by tradition and practice for centuries. The courts have not always been great champions of liberty, but as expressed by Lord Denning in a dissenting judgment in a picketing case:

'The right to demonstrate and the right to protest on matters of public concern . . . are rights which it is in the public interest that individuals should possess; and, indeed, that they should exercise without impediment so long as no wrongful act is done.'

But the Public Order Act of 1986, the first major public order statute for fifty years, has made sure that the right to demonstrate openly can be seriously restricted and controlled. It is an Act that strikes at the very heart of legitimate protest, particularly spontaneous protest. It extends existing police controls over processions and marches, it creates for the first time in the history of our law statutory controls over open-air meetings and picketing, it creates a new range of widely drawn public order offences, and it devises the first statutory offence of criminal trespass. Above all it gives the police, in the exercise of all of these powers, an almost unchallengeable discretion, described by the Prime Minister in a speech to the Conservative Party conference as 'a blank cheque'.

Police controls on marches and processions   The Public Order Act has changed the law. It provides for the first time a national requirement that organisers must give advance notice of all moving demonstrations. Failure to do so or late notice is a criminal offence. It provides new tests for imposing police controls. Before the Act the police could only impose conditions on a demonstration (for example by re-routing) where they had reasonable grounds for apprehending serious public disorder. This test has been preserved but three further alternative tests have been added. The police can now impose conditions if they anticipate serious damage to property or 'serious disruption to the life of the community' or if the purpose of the organisers is the intimidation of others. The Act also includes a wide range of offences for those who breach the police controls and conditions, in some cases carrying a penalty of imprisonment.

The test of potential disruption to the community may mean no more than that the police accept the fears of local residents that there will be noise, of local shopkeepers that the pavements will be crowded, of local motorists that the street will be blocked. The police will decide what to do. The police, either beforehand or through the senior policeman on the spot, may impose 'such conditions as they appear to him necessary', for example the reduction of numbers in the march, re-routing away from the focus point for the demonstration, or restricting the timetable. In other words the police have been given the power to take the heart out of the protest.

There is no right of appeal against the decision of the police. If they act unreasonably the decision could be challenged by way of judicial review in the High Court, but no case of judicial review against the police in this context has ever succeeded.

Police controls on assemblies   Similar restrictions are applied for the first time to open-air meetings of twenty or more persons. Parents protesting outside the town hall about inadequate child-care facilities could be removed to the local park, to 'a less sensitive area' (as the Government put it). Pickets could be reduced to two at the back gate of the factory, two at the front gate and two at the side gate. If the conditions imposed by the police are broken, criminal offences are committed.

Public order offences   The Public Order Act also sweeps away the old common law public order offences and replaces them with a new range of criminal offences. This provides a new regime of control to add to the not inconsiderable public order powers which the police already have under the law. The range of offences is from riot with a ten year maximum sentence, down through offences of violent disorder, affray and threatening behaviour to the new low level offence of disorderly conduct. At the serious end of the scale the wording of the offences is breathtaking in its vagueness. In the violent disorder offence, a catch-all charge now often used in place of more modest charges, the wording is:

> 'Where three or more persons who are present together use or threaten unlawful violence and the conduct of them (taken together) is such as would cause a person of reasonable firmness present at the scene to fear for his personal safety, each of the persons using or threatening unlawful violence is guilty of violent disorder.'

Despite the title of the offence no actual violence need take place and nobody need be present who fears for his personal safety. The maximum penalty is five years' imprisonment.

At the bottom end of the scale the Act includes the controversial new offence of disorderly conduct. It extends the criminal law into hitherto unpunished areas of annoyance, disturbance and inconvenience, covering behaviour which falls short of violence or the threat or fear of violence. It was intended to be used to protect vulnerable groups, such as the elderly. In fact it has been used quite indiscriminately, for example against juveniles for throwing fake snowballs, against a man who had a birthday party for his son in his back garden (he was charged even though he agreed to turn the music down), against two 19 year old males for kissing in the street, against a nudist on a beach and against another nudist in his own house, and, most sinisterly, in the so-called Madame M case (successfully taken up by NCCL) against four students who were in the process of putting up a satirical poster during the last general election. It depicted the Prime Minister as a sadistic dominatrix.

The Prevention of Terrorism Act (PTA)

The PTA contains extreme police powers for any democratic

country in peace time. It was described as 'draconian' by the then Labour Home Secretary, Roy Jenkins, when he introduced the Bill to Parliament shortly after the Birmingham pub bombings in 1974. But it was also intended to be a temporary measure when it was passed in a single sitting in 1974. The full title of the current Act is the Prevention of Terrorism (Temporary Provisions) Act 1984. Although the statistics on the PTA suggest that it is used harshly and often unnecessarily, and although the Police and Criminal Evidence Act 1984 has given the police new increased powers, the PTA will be renewed in 1989 and continue with its most seriously criticised provisions.

The Prevention of Terrorism Acts of 1974, 1976, 1984 (and 1989), have swept away safeguards to protect the liberty of the citizen won over centuries. By replacing legally defined and protected rights with arbitrary executive powers, the PTA violates cardinal principles of the rule of law. These are strong condemnations, but they are justified by an examination of the extraordinary powers conferred on ministers by the PTA.

The worst powers in the PTA are detention without charge for up to seven days, criminal offences for remaining silent, and exclusion orders which create a regime of internal exile. All three aspects are likely to remain in the Act when it is renewed.

Detention without charge   The police may arrest and detain without charge for up to 48 hours any person they have reasonable grounds to believe is a person guilty of belonging to a proscribed organisation or guilty of other offences under the PTA, a person who is or has been 'concerned in the commission, preparation or instigation of acts of terrorism' connected with the affairs of Northern Ireland, or a person subject to an exclusion order. Terrorism is widely defined as meaning 'the use of violence for political ends, and includes any use of violence for the purpose of putting the public or any section of the public in fear'. The Home Secretary can extend the period of detention without charge from 48 hours up to a total of seven days. During that time the person may be detained incommunicado, without legal advice for up to 48 hours and without having a friend or close relative informed of his detention.

The European Commission of Human Rights has already ruled in 1987 in the case of four Northern Irish men that a total of seven days without charge is too long. In December 1988 the ruling was confirmed by the European Court which held that four days and six hours was too long but did not stipulate an acceptable period. The

Government has shown no sign of complying with this decision by amending the Act. It could plead a formal derogation from the Court's decision on the ground that extraordinary powers are needed to safeguard the 'life of the nation'. But this would leave open the possibility of a fresh challenge in Europe, as would some form of compromise, possibly involving judicial scrutiny of individual cases. In 1983 Lord Jellicoe reported to the Government that the extensions should be approved by the Home Secretary personally. The Government rejected that proposal.

Many innocent people have been stopped and searched, some have been detained. They include Irish ministers, journalists, writers, students and hundreds with just Irish (usually Catholic Irish) connections.

Criminal offences   Section 11 of the PTA makes it an offence punishable with up to five years' imprisonment not to pass on information to the police about a future act of terrorism or about people involved in terrorism connected with the affairs of Northern Ireland. In an official report on the PTA in 1978 Lord Shackleton expressed grave doubts about Section 11, both in practical terms and on grounds of principle: 'It has an unpleasant ring about it in terms of civil liberties.' Lord Colville also recommended its repeal after his review of the Act in 1987. Section 11 remains in force. It is a dangerous precedent within the criminal law, undermining a suspect's right to remain silent during questioning (see Chapter 7 below). It can lead to suspects giving false and misleading information to obtain early release from police custody. It has been used to put pressure on victims of violence to provide information, and journalists who report on events involving paramilitaries in Northern Ireland have been threatened with prosecution under this Section by the Attorney General.

Exclusion orders   An exclusion order restricts a person to living either in Northern Ireland or in mainland Britain, a decision which can have far-reaching consequences for those concerned. It deprives them of the right to move freely around the United Kingdom and to live where they wish. Families may be divided and job prospects reduced. Some people seeking to leave Northern Ireland may even be prevented from escaping terrorist associates.

Furthermore, the procedure for making and renewing orders is a complete denial of basic rights. The decision is made by the Home Secretary or the Secretary of State for Northern Ireland after an entirely secret process. No charges are brought, there is no trial and the evidence is not tested in a court of law. No reasons are given for the decision. The subject can make representations but is not allowed to know the case he has to meet. Every three years a review is made, but the procedure is the same.

Once the order is made the subject is labelled as a terrorist. The Home Secretary notifies him that he is satisfied that he is or has been 'concerned in the commission, preparation or instigation of acts of terrorism'. That is the end of it. Sean Stitt, a Belfast student, could not travel to NUS conferences on the mainland; he could not visit his sister in England. Represented by NCCL he challenged his exclusion order in the High Court, but was told that the court could not intervene because the Government had invoked the cloak of national security. Three months later his nine year old exclusion order was dropped. No explanation was given. One day he was a terrorist, the next day he was not.

Despite a recommendation by Lord Colville in an official report in 1987 that exclusion orders should be scrapped because they were a severe infringement of civil liberties, exclusion orders will stay. At the end of 1987 112 orders were in force. The Government is determined to have every possible emergency measure at its disposal. Lord Colville was reported in *The Guardian* to have said that exclusion orders were an embarrassment to this country's reputation in the international community. He said he could no longer defend the procedure at human rights conventions and the Soviet Union were citing exclusion orders in defence of their own practices. The Home Secretary prefers to accept the police's ardent view that the power is necessary to curb terrorism: 'If we have to wait until evidence of a specific offence is available, then we may have to wait until there is a victim.'

Statistics In the first ten years of the operation of the PTA to December 1984, 5,905 people were arrested and detained in Great Britain in connection with Northern Ireland terrorism. Many more were stopped and searched. Of the 5,905, 275 people were excluded to Northern Ireland, 152 were charged with offences under the Act, 13 with conspiracy to commit offences under the Act and 294 with other offences. Of the 152 charged, the charges were dropped in 15 cases and 21 persons were acquitted. The vast majority therefore, over 85%, were neither excluded nor charged with a criminal offence. Only 7.7% were charged with any offences, including non-terrorist offences. Of those detained under the PTA in 1987 only 12% were charged with offences.

New moves against terrorists   The Government is planning a number of new legal measures intended to curb terrorism relating to the affairs of Northern Ireland. Some of these measures are included in the renewed Prevention of Terrorism Act which will become law in 1989. These are sweeping additional powers. They include new laws reversing the burden of proof in the seizure of assets, the abolition of the right of silence (see Chapter 7), and a ban on candidates in elections who do not renounce violence.

New moves to seize terrorist funds are causing concern. The new section in the PTA is likely to include a shift in the traditional burden of proof on to the defendant. Suspects will be asked to prove a negative, namely that they did not intend to spend the money in their possession on terrorism, a particularly difficult task for the innocent who could be wrongly deprived of their property. This is a dangerous precedent for the law of the United Kingdom. Once again Northern Ireland is being used as a testing ground for emergency powers which experience shows are likely to be introduced into the ordinary criminal law of the United Kingdom.

Emergency powers in Northern Ireland

The Prevention of Terrorism Act (PTA) took its powers from a long history of emergency provisions in Northern Ireland. By the time the PTA is renewed in 1989 it will already have taken over in Northern Ireland from emergency provisions as the main weapon in the controlling array of arrest and detention powers. Each year in Northern Ireland more than 1,000 people are detained under the PTA. Irish critics on both sides of the border complain that the PTA gives the police enormous power which they use more as a general trawl for low-level intelligence gathering on the Irish community (particularly the Catholic community) than a weapon against terrorist crime.

The other mainstay of police powers in Northern Ireland is the Northern Ireland (Emergency Provisions) Act (EPA). The EPA was enacted in 1973, re-enacted by a Labour Government in 1978 and amended in 1987 following the Baker Report in 1984.

Although some slight improvements were made to the EPA following the report of Sir George Baker in 1984 the Government has retained its most unsatisfactory aspects. They include wide powers of search, arrest, and detention coupled with long delays before trial, weakened rules of evidence, and the removal of juries for certain serious offences.

The EPA abolishes jury trial for 'scheduled offences' and creates the Diplock Courts in which scheduled offences are tried by judge alone. The test for exclusion of confession evidence is weaker in Northern Ireland than in England and Wales. The EPA allows confessions which were not obtained 'voluntarily' to be used in court. Confessions are only excluded if they have been obtained by torture, inhuman or degrading treatment or following violence or threats of violence. The EPA does not adopt the more flexible unreliability test for confession evidence used in England and Wales.

The EPA also retains the option of the reintroduction of internment, despite the recommendation by Baker that the power to intern without trial should be repealed. Unionist politicians in Northern Ireland called in 1988 for the reintroduction of internment of suspected IRA terrorists following a sustained campaign of IRA violence.

The Government refused to follow other recommendations of Baker including the right to automatic bail after twelve months in custody awaiting trial (the average period on remand in Northern Ireland being 178 days in 1985) and a reduction in the army's policing powers.

The EPA is still described as emergency legislation but the Government's commitment to the continuation of the EPA in the long term is shown by the change in the renewal period from every six months to twelve months. Northern Ireland has in fact experienced emergency legislation continuously for the past 67 years.

Police and Criminal Evidence Act (PACE)

It was with the backdrop of emergency powers in Northern Ireland and draconian powers in the Prevention of Terrorism Act that the Government brought forward the most important document on general police powers this century, the Police and Criminal Evidence Act of 1984. This is a major statute, designed to set the tone of policing well into the twenty-first century.

PACE, as it is commonly known, was the product of a lot of thought. It followed after the Royal Commission on Criminal Procedure had made extensive recommendations in 1981. The Royal Commission had been asked to examine police powers and the prosecution process 'having regard both to the interests of the community in bringing offenders to justice and to the rights and liberties of persons suspected or accused of crime'.

While the Commission was able to conclude in its report that it was for 'Parliament to strike the balance between the rights of the individual and the security of society', it soon became clear that the government of the day was greatly influenced by the demands of a powerful police lobby for more powers. And there was, as ever, a powerful political lobby within the Conservative Party for tougher powers to combat the tide of rising crime. The end result was indeed more powers. Even the *Daily Mail* said that PACE would give the police too much power. Unfortunately there is no sign of a corresponding fall in crime to justify these new and extensive powers.

Stop and search   Police powers to stop and search persons on the street were extended. A new power to set road blocks was introduced. The powers of search were extended as were the powers of seizure of material, without adequate safeguards to avoid abuse.

Arrest   There are two powers of arrest without warrant. They are the power of arrest for 'arrestable offences', which include all serious offences carrying a maximum prison sentence of five years, and the power of arrest for non-arrestable offences where 'general arrest conditions' are satisfied. It is this second power which gives rise to concern.

The power to arrest without warrant was given the widest possible scope by the introduction of the general arrest conditions section which in its length and complexity is barely comprehensible to the officer on the street, let alone the average member of the public. As a result it is used frequently and often unlawfully. It provides a power of arrest for any non-arrestable offence, however trivial (such as dropping litter), so long as certain minor conditions are satisfied.

If, for example, the police officer questioning someone about a non-arrestable offence simply decides that he is not satisfied about the name or address given to him, he can make an arrest. The arrested person is taken away to the police station and will be locked up until, in the exercise of further police discretion, he can be released. In the Madame M poster case (see the Public Order Act above) the police claimed that they had the power to arrest four students for putting up a poster because they were not satisfied about their addresses. But in court the police admitted that they had not even asked them for their addresses. In London and the Home

Counties the police have started arresting people for failing to pay parking tickets.

Detention　　PACE extends the right to detain suspects for up to 96 hours without charge. Sir David McNee, Metropolitan Police Commissioner at the time of the Royal Commission, had wanted the power to detain to be even longer, with an unlimited number of 72 hour extensions. The PACE provision, although severe, was in the circumstances something of a compromise. But it also left the longest extensions to be decided by a magistrates court sitting in private session, closed to the public. Lord McCluskey, debating in Parliament a similar but less drastic proposal for Scotland, commented: 'I detect shades of South Africa here, and indeed of the police state, in allowing successive periods of detention on a mere magistrate's warrant.' Longer detention also means greater reliance by the police on confession evidence, which is likely to become more unreliable the longer the detention (see right of silence, Chapter 7).

PACE also extends the powers for searching (including strip searching) suspects at the police station, and for taking fingerprints. The Act does not provide sufficiently narrow grounds for strip searching, despite a report in 1980 by the Police Complaints Board that too many strip searches were routine: 'We are left with the impression that the procedure is sometimes followed with an element of vindictiveness where a prisoner has given the arresting officers a hard time.' PACE also creates the power to make 'intimate searches' and take 'intimate samples', in other words internal examination of parts of the body such as the vagina and the anus, which may (unless they are searches for drugs) be carried out by a police constable where a senior officer considers that it is 'not practicable' for a doctor or nurse to do it.

The rights of suspects　　Against all of this are set the modest rights of suspects. They are there in the Act: the right to have someone informed of your arrest, the right to legal advice, the right to have details of the arrest and detention recorded, the right of the innocent to have fingerprints and body samples destroyed. But these so-called rights are so hedged about with exceptions and provisos that in practice they remain, as before, at the discretion of the police. They are token rights amidst a formidable array of new police powers. The draftsmen of PACE seem to have believed that getting the police to make more records, to write down more procedures, would in itself establish the rights of suspects. Either that or it was never intended to develop any semblance of balance between powers and rights.

Many of the detailed rules for police conduct are set out not in PACE itself but in Codes of Practice made under PACE. The Codes cover stop and search powers, searches of premises, the detention, treatment and questioning of suspects, and indentification procedures. But the Codes, like the Judges Rules which came before them, do not have the force of law. That means that if the police breach the provisions of the Codes the trial court is not obliged to rule the evidence inadmissible, and in practice rarely does.

The powers created by PACE have not satisfied the thirst of the police or of the Conservative grassroots for more police powers. The demands go on. The police do not like PACE anyway. They find it too complicated to understand and too cumbersome to operate. Nor have the powers in PACE reduced the incidence of crime. The statistics continue to rise. To that extent PACE has not been a success. PACE has also failed to provide adequate safeguards for suspects in custody and against the abuse of police stop and search and arrest powers.

6

Police Tactics,
Conduct and Accountability

Police tactics

It is a disturbing feature of policing in the 1980s that police officers are frequently required to perform a quasi-military role. They wear riot gear and employ tactics to match. They have the capacity to use plastic bullets and other machinery of violence, and they carry and use firearms.

The most powerful speech against turning policemen into soldiers came from Alan Wright, chairman of the Police Federation branch in Northern Ireland, in a speech to the Federation's conference in 1986. As an officer of the most heavily militarised police force in the United Kingdom, the Royal Ulster Constabulary, he was well qualified to warn against drifting into a paramilitary role and corrupting the ideal of an unarmed service.

In 1987, John Alderson, a former Chief Constable, said: 'Eventually, all the top people who have held back the tide of paramilitarism for the last ten to fifteen years will have gone. The whole nature of policing will have changed by the beginning of the next century if the trend continues.' Indeed, the present Metropolitan Police Commissioner, Sir Peter Imbert, has publicly acknowledged the necessary drift towards paramilitarism.

Public order   Much immediate violence in a public order context is sparked off by police behaviour. Very few public gatherings lead to violence, but the exercise of police powers may itself be a major cause of public disorder. Lord Scarman found that the worst disorder in London in recent times, in Brixton in 1981, was in part a reaction to police behaviour. A similar reaction in 1985 contributed to widespread inner city tension and its eruption on the streets. In the USA the Kerner Commission on civil disorder found that police behaviour was the most frequently perceived source of grievance in the black community.

On other occasions 'strong' policing has generated violence. In

1985, for example, a difficult problem over the 'Peace Convoy's' approach to Stonehenge was 'solved' by breaking up the Convoy with severe police violence both to persons and property (see Chapter 8). There has been a tendency to over-police sensitive situations where conflict is expected, and to avoid more discreet police tactics. During the miners' strike of 1984-85 demonstrations were particularly heavily policed, often to the point of provocation. The use of excessive numbers of police officers may be seen as intimidatory and lead on occasions to unnecessary violence. As John Alderson put it in 1981: 'Once we start tooling up to declare war on society, policemen become the unwitting victims of violence.'

Riot control   The modern style of policing is graphically displayed by the use of riot equipment in quasi-military manoeuvres. Authorised equipment available to police forces now includes short shields, long shields, truncheons, helmets and visors, CS gas (used in Toxteth in 1981 contary to Home Office guidelines), CR gas, water cannon and plastic bullets.

A plastic bullet is a cylinder 3.25 inches long and 1.5 inches in diameter which is fired from a gun with a range of up to 70 metres. Over most of that range its impact is in 'the severe damage region'. It is euphemistically called a PVC baton round. Fourteen people were killed in Northern Ireland by rubber and plastic bullets between 1972 and 1982 (seven of them children). In 1981 29,761 bullets were fired in Northern Ireland, according to government statistics. Plastic bullets should only be fired for defensive purposes. But in the hands of a young, frightened soldier or policeman they are often used as a pre-emptive weapon. In an inquiry for NCCL Lord Gifford recorded his own experience: 'Two police vehicles had been collecting a stolen vehicle. They drove off, but after a few yards the tow-rope snapped. Someone in the crowd of bystanders laughed. At once a policeman rushed from the front vehcle towards the crowd, and fired head-high. At that point, and only then, were missiles thrown at the police.'

As we have seen repeatedly, a power once used under 'emergency' conditions in Northern Ireland is later extended to other parts of the United Kingdom. Plastic bullets are now available for police forces other than the RUC. The High Court upheld the decision of the Northumbrian police force to arm itself with plastic bullets and CS gas without prior consent from the police authority. The Home Office sent out a circular in 1986 to all chief constables setting out a procedure for obtaining these weapons without the police authority's approval. The previous Metropolitan Police Commissioner, Sir Kenneth Newman, when in office, 'warned' the people of London that he would not shrink from using plastic bullets 'for restoring peace and preventing crime and injury'.

A secret manual of riot tactics drawn up by the Association of Chief Police Officers (ACPO) revealed the nature of approved police manoeuvres. It described in detail how baton charges might disperse crowds, how a short shield and baton carrying team might 'incapacitate missile throwers and ring leaders by striking in a controlled manner with batons about the arms and legs or torso', how battle cries and the rhythmic beating of shields with truncheons should be used, and how mounted police might disperse a crowd 'using impetus and weight to create fear and a scatter effect' by advancing into the crowd at a canter. In July 1988 a Glasgow court awarded damages to two persons trapped when a 'malicious' police cavalry charge went into a street packed with football fans.

These tactics of high profile policing coupled with wide discretionary police powers, have sometimes caused resentment, frustration and even violence from otherwise peaceful members of the public.

Arming the police   Although the number of police operations in which firearms have been issued has fallen in recent years, the actual use of firearms has risen, causing an increase in public anxiety.

Police forces and specialist units are also arming themselves against all eventualities. In the wake of the Hungerford shootings a report by an HM Inspector of Constabulary to the Home Secretary recommended an increase in police mobile armed response units with armour-plated Land Rovers, similar to those used by the RUC in Northern Ireland. Armed response units have already been established in Northamptonshire and West Yorkshire, and other forces are considering following suit.

In a different context sub-machine guns were seen for the first time at Heathrow following the massacres by terrorists at airports at Rome and Vienna in 1985.

But mistakes have been made with firearms, and with serious consequences. Steven Waldorf was shot and seriously wounded in 1982. John Shorthouse was killed and Cherry Groce crippled in 1985. They were all accidental victims of the growth in the use of firearms by the police.

It is an extraordinary fact that there is no legislation on the use of firearms by the police. In 1987 the Home Office Working Group on

Police Use of Firearms considered surprisingly that an amendment to the Police and Criminal Evidence Act was 'inappropriate'. This leaves a secret document, the Association of Chief Police Officers' 1983 Manual of Guidance, as the single authoritative source of guidance on tactical and operational matters relating to the use of firearms by the police. Home Office 'Guidelines for the Police on the Issue and Use of Firearms' merely provide a few short statements of principle as the framework within which the ACPO Manual operates.

The emphasis has subtly shifted. The police no longer pretend that they do not use firearms. They now seek public acceptance, but without public accountability, by relying on their self-proclaimed high standards of expertise and training.

The Stalker affair

During November and December 1982, in three separate incidents, six police suspects were shot dead by the Royal Ulster Constabulary (RUC). Five of the men were unarmed. Three unloaded pre-war rifles were found near the sixth. The circumstances prompted allegations that the RUC was operating a 'shoot to kill' policy, ignoring elementary principles of justice. The shootings were investigated by members of the RUC and the files were sent to the Director of Public Prosecutions (DPP).

Four members of the RUC were prosecuted for murder. All were acquitted. A judge who acquitted three of them praised them for bringing the dead IRA men 'to the final court of justice'. The trials did reveal, however, that the defendants had been instructed by senior police officers to lie in their official statements in order to conceal the nature of the special police operations.

In 1984 John Stalker, then Deputy Chief Constable of Manchester, was appointed to investigate the circumstances of the shootings and the subsequent conduct of members of the RUC. He was not asked to investigate whether a 'shoot to kill' policy existed. In September 1985 Stalker submitted an interim report recommending the prosecution of 11 police officers. In his report he asked for access to a secret tape recording which he believed 'would have supported further charges against other police officers of perjury and possibly murder and attempted murder'.

Before he was able to complete his inquiry Stalker was suddenly removed from the job. This followed upon unexpected allegations about his behaviour, of which he was later exonerated. His inquiry was taken over by Colin Sampson, Chief Constable of West Yorkshire. Stalker claims that he was taken off the job because senior civil servants and policemen in Belfast could not cope with the scandal his report would create. In his book *Stalker* he says he was removed by James Anderton, his Chief Constable, in secret combination with top brass in London: 'I believe . . . I was hurriedly removed because I was on the threshold of causing a major police scandal and political row that would have resulted in several resignations and general mayhem.'

Neither the Stalker nor the Sampson reports have been made public. But Stalker himself later wrote: 'The circumstances of those shootings pointed to a police inclination, if not a policy, to shoot suspects dead without warning rather than to arrest them.' He also claims that Sir John Hermon, Chief Constable of the RUC, 'obstructed' his attempts to obtain the secret tape recording.

In early 1988 the Attorney General announced to the House of Commons that there would be no further prosecutions in respect of the six shootings. He also announced that, although evidence had been found which would have justified the prosecution of RUC officers for perverting the course of justice, the DPP had decided not to prosecute for reasons of 'public interest' and 'national security'.

These events severely undermined public confidence in the police and the administration of justice in Northern Ireland. But that was the end of the Stalker affair, at least from the Government's point of view. Obstruction, criminal activities, and ultimately secrecy prevailed.

The Gibraltar Inquest

An inquest is a narrow inquiry into a death. It is not a trial of those who caused the death. Still less is it a public inquiry dealing with all the issues directly concerning the death. One of the issues in Gibraltar was whether British soldiers were operating a 'shoot to kill' policy against terrorists.

The inquest into the deaths of three members of the IRA was held in Gibraltar in September 1988. Mairead Farrell, Danny McCann and Sean Savage had been shot dead by SAS soldiers after entering Gibraltar from Spain. According to the security services they were planning to explode a massive bomb. After lengthy deliberations, and some disagreement, the inquest jury entered a majority verdict (9-2) of lawful killing. The only other verdict available to them, on the coroner's directions, was unlawful killing.

The Government may believe that the verdict vindicates its denial of a 'shoot to kill' policy, at least in this case. But a narrow inquiry leaves important questions unanswered, notably in difficult areas of policy. The political question is to what extent the Government (at the highest level) was involved in deciding the ground rules for this operation.

The practical question is whether the decision to involve the SAS amounts inevitably to a 'shoot to kill' policy. Even assuming that the 'botched job' assessment of the shootings is correct, once the operation had passed from surveillance to action was it inevitable that the terrorists would not survive. Could the victims have been arrested rather than killed? Were the victims given a warning and an opportunity to surrender before being shot? Was there no alternative?

The rules for the use of firearms by the police are based on the United Kingdom's law of 'reasonable force', to prevent crime or to effect a lawful arrest (Section 3 Criminal Law Act 1967). But when it came to the shooting, the key question was whether the lethal force used did amount to reasonable force. The SAS soldiers shot to kill. They shot Savage in a 'frenzied' attack, according to a pathologist. They were mistaken, or badly informed, about the absence of weapons on the terrorists, the absence of detonators in their possession, and the absence of a bomb in the car parked by Savage. Was it 'reasonable force' in the circumstances?

A survey by the Irish Information Partnership of action involving the SAS between 1981 and 1986 claims to show that out of ten incidents fourteen paramilitaries and two civilians were killed but only three prisoners were taken.

Is 'reasonable force' the right test? Article 2 of the European Convention of Human Rights states that no more force shall be used than is 'absolutely necessary'. In other words, does the law provide adequate protection by European standards against the excessive use of force by the police, the army or the security services?

Other questions remain unanswered. Did the Government deliberately mount a smear campaign against the Thames Television programme *Death on the Rock* and those taking part in the programme who did not favour the SAS version of events? Was the Gibraltar police force the right body to investigate the killings when it had played such a key role in the affair?

These are not idle questions. Some partisan observers abroad have formed the image of British 'death squads' at work. The shootings were at the very least an embarrassment to the Government. One thing, however, is clear. The inquest was no substitute for a thorough public inquiry. Inquests have been found to be unsatisfactory inquiries in difficult cases. such as those concerning Blair Peach, Helen Smith, James Kelly, Roberto Calvi and the Deptford house fire. They are more than just unsatisfactory when they involve the wider issues of the rule of law.

Police misconduct

The greater the powers given to the police the greater the need for the highest integrity of serving police men and women. The abuse of power by police officers is the most serious infringement of individual liberty. It strikes at the very heart of freedom. Not even the slightest level of abuse can be excused for whatever reason. The abuse of liberty endangers liberty itself.

The bad apple theory, that there will always be one rotten apple in every barrel, was expounded by Sir Robert Mark when he was Metropolitan Police Commissioner in the mid 1970s. The theory affirmed the common assumption that the police are above suspicion, that their conduct on the whole is exemplary and that criticism of the police or policing is inspired solely by malice and left-wing activists.

The truth is, of course, to the contrary. Police misconduct exists, and the desire to eradicate it and to protect its victims is healthy and necessary.

Senior police officers, desk-bound with policy considerations and far removed from the reality of everyday policing, constantly fail to understand that many valid court cases are lost because police officers blatantly and routinely break the rules. When the codes of detention or interrogation or relating to juveniles or the mentally handicapped are broken, juries often acquit.

Sometimes, it seems, they acquit defendants merely to show disapproval of police conduct, even where there is other evidence to support the prosecution. Tainted evidence often tips the balance in the defendant's favour. As a result senior police officers and politicians complain that the acquittal rate is too high and that the rules, such as the right of silence, should be changed to favour the police and the prosecution.

Police violence   One of the worst forms of abuse is police violence. The violence may take place out of sight of members of the public, sometimes in a police van. If the victim retaliates or even acts in self-defence the police may bring retaliatory charges, particularly where the defendant receives injuries. There may be charges of assaulting or obstructing a constable in the execution of his duty, charges which can only be tried in the magistrates' court where the bench can normally be expected to convict. The evidence at court will come from two or three police officers, often their word against the defendant. If he has a criminal record, under the law it may be exposed to the court by his allegations of police misconduct.

Of those police officers involved in individual acts of violence few are caught. Some are disciplined, a handful are taken to court. The Director of Prosecutions is reluctant to prosecute except in strong cases. It is common knowledge in the courts that although juries may 'punish' police evidence when it is part of the prosecution case, they are also prepared to give police officers the benefit of the doubt when they are in the dock. The acquittal rate for police officers is high.

Nevertheless, in a twelve month period from 1987-88, a number of police officers were convicted of violence. Two Lancashire police officers were gaoled for life for the 'cowardly and brutal' murder of a drunken man at Morecambe police station. Witnesses had described how the unconscious victim had been dragged to a cell being hit with truncheons and kicked. These were the longest sentences in recent years, although the year before a Merseyside police officer had been gaoled for seven years for manslaughter. Also in that year five Metropolitan Police officers received up to four years' imprisonment for their involvement in a 'fun' attack on five schoolboys (two of them black) in the Holloway Road in North London. On the same day in the same court (the Old Bailey), but in another case, an 'outstanding' policeman was sentenced for beating up a defenceless prisoner in a police van.

Two policemen were convicted at Newcastle upon Tyne of beating up three Chelsea fans in a police van after a football match. They were convicted of wounding and also, with a third officer, of perjury and attempting to pervert the course of justice in claiming that the fans had attacked them. A police constable was convicted of kicking a person in the head at a football match. A policeman was gaoled in Sheffield for attacking a man who taunted him in the street. An award-winning constable in Derbyshire was convicted of striking a 16 year old boy 'to teach him a lesson'. It is also right to point out that assaults on police officers are up substantially in number (in London by 33%), but this can provide no justification for police violence.

In March 1985 a visit by Leon Brittan, the Home Secretary, to

Manchester University ended in chaos and injury, when the police tried without warning to clear the steps of the union building. According to a report by the Police Complaints Authority there were errors of judgment by two senior police officers and excessive force was used on demonstrators by subordinates. One student, Sarah Hollis, had been rendered unconscious. Other students complained of perjured evidence in police prosecutions. Two constables were charged with perjury and acquitted. Another student, Steven Shaw, who was involved in a private inquiry into the policing of the Brittan visit, complained of subsequent harassment and assaults by police officers. He made a formal police complaint and was later charged with attempting to pervert the course of justice. In May 1988 the Senate of Manchester University agreed unanimously to ask the Director of Public Prosecutions to reconsider the charges. Only a month earlier, a man who claimed that the police had asked him to burgle Sarah Hollis's flat and who was charged with conspiring to pervert the course of justice had been acquitted.

Charges of assault have been recommended against some police officers who policed the Rupert Murdoch dispute at Wapping in January 1987. Many who attended the mass demonstration had complained of violent and indiscriminate behaviour by certain officers. Kate Adie, the BBC journalist, made a complaint that she had been struck over the head by a police truncheon. More than 400 official complaints from members of the public led to an inquiry by the Northamptonshire police.

In September 1988 viewers of HTV's *Wales at Six* news bulletin were shocked to see police officers apparently dragging a man out of a car on Anglesey and beating him without resistance.

Complaints against the police

Despite the seriousness of many allegations of police misconduct and the volume of complaints against the police, the police complaints system is inadequate and unsatisfactory. In 1987 the Police Complaints Authority (PCA), which was set up under the Police and Criminal Evidence Act 1984, received some 13,147 complaints against the police (allegations of assault formed the majority of them). Only 156 disciplinary charges were brought against police officers as a result of those complaints. Even when complaints are substantiated, the complainant receives no compensation and may not even receive an apology.

Statistics show that fewer than 10% of complaints will be upheld.

In the Metropolitan Police area the figure is as low as 3%. Home Office research has shown that a black complainant has three times less chance of success in making a complaint than a white complainant. Complainants often say that pressure is put upon them by the investigating officer to withdraw their complaint. As many as 40-50% of all recorded complaints are subsequently 'withdrawn'. In Steven Shaw's case (above) his formal complaints led to his being charged with attempting to pervert the course of justice. Every complainant is also at risk of being sued for defamation by the individual officer who may be backed by the Police Federation.

Even though the PCA introduces some independent element of control over the inquiry into police complaints, the investigation of the complaint is still carried out by police officers. The PCA has expressed fears that police officers close ranks over inquiries and give false evidence to protect each other. The present Metropolitan Police Commissioner, Sir Peter Imbert, has recognised publicly that there is some scepticism about the genuine independence of the PCA.

In the Holloway Road incident (above) it took political pressure from outside to break over three years of silence. The PCA has also recorded its concern about the 'inordinate delay' which some police forces have been guilty of in responding to complaints: 'It has appeared to the authority [the PCA] that forces are trying every conceivable tactic to dissuade the authority from pressing charges.'

For these reasons the complaints procedure has generally failed to inspire public confidence. Would-be complainants are therefore turning to the civil courts for a remedy.

Civil actions against the police   Civil actions against the police have a higher success rate than official police complaints. The country-wide figures show on average a greater than 30% success rate. In London the figures for 1986 show a 49% success rate. The complainant has the added advantage over a police complaint in that success will bring financial compensation. The courts award damages for the torts (civil wrongs) of assault, false imprisonment, malicious prosecution and other torts.

In London the number of police complaints dropped from 9,178 in 1981 to 5,462 in 1985. By comparison payments in civil actions against the police rose in the same period from £31,871 to £377,158, the latter figure comprising £330,322 in out of court settlements and £46,836 in awards by the courts.

In recent years there have been a number of reported cases against the police. A Greenham Common peace campaigner won damages for a strip search by Ministry of Defence police. The estate of Blair Peach, a teacher who was killed allegedly by police during a National Front demonstration in 1979, was paid £75,000 by the Metropolitan Police. £200,000 was awarded to Barry Carliell after he lost an eye as a result of a punch by a police officer in a police station. Karl Kelly was paid £20,000 by the Metropolitan Police in an out of court settlement. He claimed that he had been wrongly arrested and falsely charged five times in two years. Derek Gordon was paid £15,000 by the West Midlands Police after he was charged and detained for a murder he did not commit. He had allegedly made a false confession while in police custody. Tony Diedrick, a black man, was awarded £1,700 by a judge for suffering 'indignity and humiliation' at the hands of the police in London. He needed hospital treatment for his injuries. Kathleen Gibbons, aged 76, was awarded £1,200 by a judge who found she had been falsely imprisoned, assaulted and maliciously prosecuted by London police for selling a miners' newspaper outside a bookshop. A photographer received damages for an unnecessary strip search. A police officer was awarded damages against the police for his wrongful arrest in a public lavatory.

Police accountability and local authorities

The police should be accountable through an effective police complaints system and in serious cases of misconduct by way of compensation in the civil courts. They should also be accountable for their policing policies through democratically elected bodies. Regrettably, the only body which contains a democratic element, the police authority, has been emaciated by central government control.

As long ago as 1962 the Royal Commission on the Police recognised that the balance between local and central government was shifting: 'A realistic appraisal of the present arrangements for control must consequently recognise that for many years there has been, under the guidance of Home departments, a centralising process which has steadily gained momentum. As a result the police service cannot with any precision be described simply as a local service . . . Much of the evidence we heard indicated that the influence of the central Government is now dominant'. More recently, Sir Kenneth Newman, when Metropolitan Police Commissioner, expressed the view in 1987: 'Looking to the future, there will come a time when in spite of people's dislike of a national police agency, if we are to be effective in dealing with organised crime we are going to have to have something in the nature of an FBI.'

This shift in favour of centralised control has meant the inevitable weakening of police authorities. The little power that police authorities had in the past has been whittled away almost completely by the Government's break-up of the traditional tripartite structure of policing. This structure which holds responsibility for the police is set out in the Police Act 1964. It comprises the police, the Home Secretary and the police authority. The Act gives 'direction and control' of the force to the chief constable but makes the authority responsible for an 'adequate and efficient' force. The Home Secretary's role is less clear. He alone is the police authority for London and he has considerable influence over policy making. In a case about the supply of plastic bullets to a police force without the consent of the police authority (see above), the High Court ruled that the Home Secretary had a statutory power to override the wishes of police authorities.

The tripartite structure ought to provide true accountability. But it has failed to do so. First, the law itself is inadequate. It has never given police authorities sufficient powers to make the tripartite structure a reality. A police authority is not permitted by law (Police Act 1964) to act like any other council committee, with the chief officer advising the committee and implementing its decisions. As the Royal Commission on the Police expressed it: 'In the case of the police these positions will be reversed. The role of the police authority will be to advise the chief constable on general matters connected with the policing of the area, but decisions will be the responsibility of the chief constable alone.' Or as James Anderton, Chief Constable of Greater Manchester and ACPO President, put it (in May 1987): 'We are accountable, I suppose, essentially to ourselves as a responsible body.'

Secondly, in the miner's strike of 1984-85 the Government took the opportunity to break down the tripartite structure, such as it was. When some police authorities attempted to use their limited powers over budgets to influence local policing, the Home Secretary threatened them with court action. Police authorities were exposed as the weakest partner in the triumvirate. They found that they had no power or control over their police forces.

Meanwhile there was evidence to suggest that the Home Office, although it denied it, was playing a part giving national directions through the National Reporting Centre (NRC). The NRC is the ad hoc centre which is managed by the senior members of the

Association of Chief Police Officers (ACPO). It is 'activated' when it is judged that police forces in more than one area are likely to require reinforcements. In the miners' strike the NRC was actively involved, with at least some level of co-operation from the Home Office, in managing the anti-strike campaign. This raised the suspicion that ACPO, which is not accountable to Parliament, was being used by the Government as a political weapon to defeat the strike.

Thirdly, the abolition in 1985 of the six Metropolitan Counties (and the Greater London Council), mostly run by parties in opposition to the Government, silenced a particularly vociferous group of police authorities. They were beginning to exert some influence at a local level and to create interest amongst other police authorities who had not felt able to have a say in local police policy before. The Metropolitan authorities have now been replaced by undemocratic joint boards (for police, fire and passenger transport), which are made up of councillors nominated by district councils.

London has never had a local, elected police authority at all. The Home Secretary is the sole police authority for the Metropolitan Police.

Just as the Government reduced the right to vote by abolishing the GLC and the Metropolitan authorities, it also succeeded in removing any hope for a democratic say in local policing. The pretence of the tripartite structure has gone. Serious policing issues continue to be decided through the structures of central government and by the autocracy of chief constables.

7

Criminal Justice

The criminal justice system is in urgent need of reform: to ensure fair and speedy trials, to improve the efficiency of the courts, to give practical effect to the independence of the prosecution service, to provide a more effective process for dealing with miscarriages of justice, to reduce prison overcrowding, to provide better alternatives to custody, and to institute a fair system for prisoners' grievances and discipline.

Rising crime (particularly violent crime and sexual offences), more criminal cases, more police officers and more demands by senior police officers and senior judges for changes in the rules, have led to a hardening of attitudes on the criminal justice system. The rights of suspects (as we have seen in Chapter 5) and the rights of defendants have been forced to take a very secondary position.

The Crown Prosecution Service

The Crown Prosecution Service (CPS) was introduced in 1986 following a recommendation by the Royal Commission on Criminal Procedure (see Chapter 5). It takes, quite rightly, the business of prosecuting suspects out of the hands of the police and places it in the hands of an organisation headed by the Director of Public Prosecutions. Unfortunately, this body started off in chaos, with a lack of funds and staff. It lacked efficiency and the ability to make decisions on prosecutions independently from the police, thus avoiding one of the cardinal principles behind its creation. Too many cases are taken to court which should never have been brought.

Secret hearings

Since the introduction of wider contempt powers by the Contempt of Court Act 1981, there has been a worrying tendency of judges to hold more court hearings in private session, closed to public scrutiny. Private justice behind closed doors is rarely necessary in the criminal courts. These powers should be sparingly used.

Both Crown Courts and magistrates courts have extended secret hearings beyond normal reporting restrictions. The press and the public have been excluded from trials. Defendants' names and addresses have been withheld, for example the address of an MP charged with a motoring offence. Witnesses have given evidence without having to reveal their names. Banning orders have been made to prevent publication of specific information.

All of this has taken place without any right of appeal, that is until the Government was forced to provide one in the Criminal Justice Act 1988 as a result of a 'friendly settlement' (see Chapter 9) of cases in Europe. NCCL took two cases to the European Commission of Human Rights. One case was on behalf of the National Union of Journalists. Tim Crook, a journalist at the Old Bailey, had been prevented from reporting the name of a witness, Miss X, because it would have caused 'distress to her and her family'. In the other case Channel Four had been prevented from re-enacting the exact words of the Clive Ponting trial (see Chapter 3) day by day.

Sometimes the police and prosecution service take advantage of the development of secrecy. One judge criticised the police for trying to close the doors on a hearing in which the police were demanding that the press hand over photographs taken at Wapping during the News International dispute. In a recent civil case a judge heard the case in private because the mother of a child who was awarded damages for medical negligence did not want to receive begging letters. The judge later admitted that he had been in error. Magistrates in some parts of the country refused to identify themselves to the press and journalists and newspapers have had to take them to the High Court to establish a more open policy.

Trial by jury under attack

Financial expediency   Although the principle of jury trial is firmly established under the law, erosion of the principle has taken place on the grounds of cost and expediency. This has been achieved by removing specific offences from the list of cases triable in the Crown Court. This trend started under a Labour Government in 1975 when the James Committee recommended the redistribution of business between the Crown Court and magistrates courts. The first to go were offences of criminal damage where the value was low (but since then increased to £2,000), drink driving offences, and homosexual soliciting.

The latest offences to go (under the Criminal Justice Act 1988) are the offences of common assault, taking motor vehicles without authority and driving while disqualified. An estimated 10,000 defendants a year will be affected. All these offences carry the possibility of a prison sentence and, in the case of driving offences, disqualification from driving which may lead to loss of livelihood. Another effect of taking these cases off the list is to remove the defendant's right to advance disclosure of the prosecution's case, to know the case that has to be met.

The expediency argument seems to find favour, albeit at the expense of principle. The Lord Chancellor, Lord Mackay, has said that the workload of Crown Courts must be reduced to cut delays and improve efficiency. As the James Committee pointed out, trial by jury is much more expensive than summary trial. There is also a severe shortage of Crown Court judges (but not of volunteer magistrates), so severe that senior officials in the Lord Chancellor's Department believe that the only way to cope with the problem is to reduce further the right to trial by jury. In 1987 the Crown Courts handled a record 135,957 cases; 404 judges handled more then 97,000 criminal trials.

Senior judges including Lord Lane, the Lord Chief Justice, are pressing for further reductions, particularly of the right to trial by jury for cases of theft of small value. So far this has been resisted by the Government because it is recognised that a conviction for dishonesty, however small the value, is a serious blight on a person's character. Other offences under consideration are burglary, soft drugs and offensive weapons (an offence which has been extended by the Criminal Justice Act 1988 to cover the carrying in public of any knife except a small folding penknife).

In 1985 the Roskill Committee, with Lord Lane's support, called for the abolition of juries in serious fraud cases. But no action has as yet been taken on this recommendation.

The Diplock Courts   In Northern Ireland the Government has continued to support the retention of the Diplock Courts and the trial of 'scheduled offences' without a jury (see Chapter 5).

Using the example of Northern Ireland, Lord Lane called in 1983 for serious consideration to be given to removing the right of trial by jury in England and Wales in cases such as large robbery cases where jury nobbling had 'become prevalent'. Lord Lane said: 'If, as in the case of terrorist trials in Northern Ireland, it becomes the only way in which criminals can be brought to justice, then there may be no alternative.'

Peremptory challenge   Another attack on jury trial has come with the removal by the Criminal Justice Act 1988 of the right of peremptory challenge. Peremptory challenge was an important feature of trial by jury. It allowed a defendant to challenge a limited number of jurors without having to give a reason. The right of peremptory challenge had been criticised as permitting the defence in multiple defendant cases to pack juries with sympathetic looking jurors. In practice, however, the right provided the defendant with an important safeguard against a jury which appeared to be neither random nor impartial in its composition. Furthermore, Home Office statistics released in January 1987 failed to show any correlation between the use of challenges and a higher rate of acquittal.

Peremptory challenge gave, for example, a black defendant the right to challenge an all-white jury. This would usually create only token black representation on the jury, but it could inspire greater confidence in the 'random' jury. The abolition of peremptory challenge will undoubtedly encourage lengthy arguments at court in support of challenges 'for cause'. In 1977 the right of peremptory challenge was reduced from seven to three jurors. Now it has been abolished altogether.

The right of silence

The Government has finally come clean on the right of silence: it will be abolished. The announcement was made by the Home Secretary in October 1988. First it has been abolished in Northern Ireland, the usual testing ground for experimentation. Then it is to be abolished in England and Wales, a decision which pre-empts the findings of a Home Office Working Party which is not due to report until early 1989.

The prosecution will be able to draw a jury's attention to a defendant's silence at the police station or in court (if he declines to give evidence) and to invite the jury to draw adverse inferences from that silence. It is the end of one of the longest surviving safeguards for the innocent suspect.

The right of silence is the right to be protected against self-incrimination. It is the right not to answer questions and not to make a response in the face of an allegation of crime. It is reflected in this country (and also in the USA) by the words of the police caution.

The police must say the words of the caution at the time of arrest, before an interview and after charge: 'You do not have to say anything unless you wish to do so, but what you say may be given in evidence.'

Protective role   There are two fundamental aspects to the right of silence. The first lies in its protective role. The value of the right of silence is the protection it gives to the weak, the frightened, the confused, the inarticulate, the mentally handicapped, or to any person who may be tempted to give an inaccurate, a partial, a misleading, even a false account of events, possibly to protect a third party, but still be innocent of the crime. It is all the more important when the suspect does not know the full nature of the allegation against him. Police officers often deliberately conceal evidence in their possession in questioning suspects.

The right of silence is a protection against oppressive questioning by police officers who believe they know best. It is a protection against false confessions, made to escape the clutches of eager and effective interrogators.

In a report on the Broadwater Farm cases which arose out of the riot on an estate in North London in 1985 and the murder of PC Blakelock, Amnesty International questioned the fairness of the trials. It concluded that detained suspects, including juveniles, were denied access to lawyers and family during lengthy periods of police interrogation. One 13 year old confessed after three days. He was interrogated wearing only his pants and a blanket. The trial judge said his treatment was unlawful and oppressive. His confession, the only evidence against him, was ruled inadmissible. Doubt existed, Amnesty said, about the safety of convictions based on contested statements made in the absence of a lawyer. In December 1988 the Court of Appeal ruled that the convictions of three men for the murder of PC Blakelock were 'safe and satisfactory' despite resting entirely on confession evidence.

In August 1988 a conviction was quashed by the Court of Appeal because the police interrogation of an educationally subnormal teenager was so irregular that the admissions he made should not have been put before the jury. In February 1988 a prosecution for a double murder was dropped against a young millworker when another man pleaded guilty to the murders. The only evidence against the millworker had been an oral confession made in the absence of a solicitor.

· It should also be remembered that the Royal Commission on

Criminal Procedure was set up after an inquiry into the Maxwell Confait case, a particularly bad case of false confessions and breaches of the rules of interrogations. The Commission came down strongly in favour of retaining the right of silence.

Furthermore, suspects are all too often deprived of the presence of a solicitor or independent third person to monitor the interview for fairness. The exceptions provided by statute to a suspect's right to see a solicitor are so widely drawn (see Chapter 5) that the police regularly deny access. The tape recording of interviews, which gives some protection and is undoubtedly the most effective way for the prosecution of presenting confession evidence, is still relatively rare. Removing the right of silence, or even diluting it, will place undue emphasis on the value of police interrogation while deflecting the police from the need to search for evidence independent of the suspect.

Presumption of innocence   The second fundamental aspect to the right of silence is that it reflects the overriding principle of our system of justice, the presumption of innocence. The abolition of the right of silence will shift the emphasis of the burden of proof from the prosecution to the defendant. As Leon Brittan, a former Home Secretary, commented: 'That rule of law is not just a procedural nicety. It is a fundamental bulwark on which our freedom rests.' And as Brittan pointed out, it would not be the professional criminal who would lose out, because he would always be ready with his answers.

The value of the right of silence to a fair system of justice is much misunderstood by the general public. The Government is taking advantage of that ignorance by deploying the 'fight against terrorism' argument to justify this retrograde step. Only 4% take advantage of the right to remain silent. It is therefore wrong to suggest that its abolition will affect rising crime. In Singapore, the right was abolished in 1976. Research there shows that abolition has not helped the police at all. The right of silence must be retained.

Documents and hearsay evidence

Another dangerous change in the trial process concerns the use of documents. The Government's concern to remove any difficulties in getting documentary evidence into court has led to the introduction (in the Criminal Justice Act 1988) of rules of evidence which will allow documents to speak for themselves. This has very serious

66

implications. It will permit dubious hearsay evidence. A police officer will be able, for example, to say: 'The witness is too frightened to attend trial, so I have taken a statement from him and this is what he says.' The statement then becomes evidence of fact just as if the person had given live evidence. This is a serious inroad into the fundamental principle that criminal trials should proceed by way of oral evidence unless all parties agree.

Extradition

In the Criminal Justice Act 1988 the Government abolished the so-called *prima facie* rule in extradition proceedings. The Home Secretary is now allowed to waive by Order in Council the need for any particular country to show that it has sufficient *(prima facie)* evidence to warrant a trial before extraditing someone from the United Kingdom.

This change affects the traditional safeguards afforded to political refugees in this country. It permits extradition on flimsy evidence where the request by the foreign power is politically motivated. It permits the Home Secretary to make decisions about refugees as a result of pressure by foreign governments. It removes a minimum safeguard, consistent with the evidence required for committal for trial, and therefore provides for inequality before the law.

The move was opposed by the Criminal Bar Association, the organisation Justice and the Chief Metropolitan Stipendiary Magistrate. They all argued that the existing *prima facie* rule should be retained so that the courts could continue to scrutinise openly and fully any request for extradition.

Judges

Judges are appointed by the Lord Chancellor from practising lawyers, mostly barristers. They are not elected. They do not emerge at the top through a carefully structured system of professional judges. They are also quite capable of making heavily weighted decisions in politically sensitive cases.

The most striking examples were seen during the miners' strike of 1984-85. Serious infringements of civil liberties were passed over: the denial of freedom of movement by stopping Kent miners from passing through the Dartford Tunnel, the denial of the right to protest by stopping miners from picketing, the denial of justice by permitting magistrates courts to impose standard bail terms with punitive conditions, the abuse of the prosecution process in starting massive public order trials on shaky evidence. These are just a few examples of the principles which fell by the wayside in cases that went to court.

Appeals

There is continuing disquiet at the number of possible wrongful convictions and the narrowness of the appeal procedure to deal with miscarriages of justice. Organisations like Justice and NCCL receive many cases claiming wrongful conviction. Some of the more dramatic cases have been highlighted in programmes on television such as *Rough Justice*; others struggle to get the attention they deserve.

An already overstretched Court of Appeal has had to formulate since its inception in 1907 a series of strict rules to protect itself from a flood of appeals. The narrow view taken by the Court of its powers is understandable. It prefers to deal with mistakes of law or defects of process rather than questions of innocence. In particular the narrow interpretation of 'fresh evidence' and the development of the 'lurking doubt' approach to the correctness of a conviction need to be reappraised.

At the same time successive Home Secretaries have shown a marked unwillingness to exercise their power to refer cases back to the Court of Appeal, and those cases which have been referred back have proved the Court to be a reluctant instrument for providing redress.

Amnesty International has concluded, and NCCL concurs, that the case of the six men convicted of the Birmingham pub bombings, whose appeal against conviction was dismissed by the Court of Appeal in January 1988, should not be closed. It believes that grave doubts remain about the official denials of ill-treatment of the prisoners in police custody.

The system will be further tested by two important cases: the appeals of the Hickey cousins and a third man against their conviction for the murder of Carl Bridgewater in 1978, and the case of the three men and a woman convicted of the 1974 Guildford and Woolwich pub bombings, a case which the Home Secretary has ordered the police to investigate further.

A new approach to possible miscarriages of justice is clearly required. The only change made by the Criminal Justice Act 1988 is to increase the Court of Appeal's powers to order a retrial after quashing a conviction, a power which will expose the defendant to double jeopardy and prolong an already lengthy process.

Sentencing

Longer sentences   Despite constant calls in the press and elsewhere for tougher sentences, the statistics show that sentences overall are in fact getting longer. According to the National Association for the Care and Resettlement of Offenders (NACRO) the average length of sentence passed rose from 16.4 months imprisonment in 1983 to 18 months in 1986. Council of Europe figures show that, in almost every year, this country sends more people to prison than any other country in Europe per head of population. Between 1980 and 1986 the number of juveniles sentenced to long periods of detention for serious crimes doubled. This is not a record to be proud of. Furthermore the alternatives to prison are inadequate and poorly funded. New gimmicks like electronic tagging are no substitute for constructive alternatives.

Prosecution appeals   The Court of Appeal has been given a new power to review and increase sentences. If the Attorney General considers that a particular sentence is 'unduly lenient' he may refer the case to the Court of Appeal. This new law (under the Criminal Justice Act 1988) was passed despite the fears that the Attorney General, who wears both a legal and a political hat, will be pressured to refer cases as a result of the outcry whipped up in certain newspapers. The Attorney General will be drawn into the process of prosecution and the defendant will be placed in double jeopardy.

Prisons and prisoners

Longer sentences and more people being sent to prison per head of population than any other country in Europe (see above) has resulted in grossly overcrowded prisons. Despite some prison building and the conversion of army barracks as temporary prisons, many prisons remain, as they have for decades, overfull institutions with appalling conditions. In his annual report for 1987, Judge Stephen Tumin, the HM Chief Inspector of Prisons, said that the prison service was 'creaking under severe stress' from overcrowding, undermanning and low staff morale.

Recent governments have shown little commitment to reducing the prison population and in improving conditions in prisons.

Despite recent widespread unrest, rioting and the taking of hostages, the Government has also shown little interest in the reform of prisoners' grievance procedures and the internal disciplinary system.

Overcrowding   In 1966 a Prison department report warned of the implications of prison overcrowding in terms of 'the human need for sufficient living space to provide both privacy and shared activities'. In 1975 the prison population stood at 40,500. The then Home Secretary, Roy Jenkins, said that if it rose to 42,000 'conditions in the system would approach the intolerable and drastic action to relieve the position would be inescapable'. In October 1976 that figure was reached and has been rising ever since. The 50,000 mark has long since been surpassed. It is estimated that on present trends the population in 1995 could be as high as 67,000.

One of the ironies of overcrowding is that those who commit more serious crimes and therefore receive longer sentences end up with better conditions. Overcrowding is concentrated in the local prisons, where the remand prisoners and the short-term prisoners are housed.

Unconvicted prisoners   The proportion of all defendants on remand in custody awaiting trial has tripled since the 1950s and doubled since the Bail Act was passed in 1976 (with the intention of letting out more suspects on bail pending trial). In the 1950s the proportion of remand prisoners in custody was 6%. For ten years before the Bail Act the figure was 9%. Now the figure is 18%. This means that not only are more people being sentenced to prison; more people are also being sent to prison before trial. Only about 4% of defendants granted bail fail to attend their trial, but the percentage of those on bail is declining. There is also widespread divergence in the bail-custody figures on a geographical basis. In early 1987 the bail figure for Greater Manchester was 65%, compared with a figure of 99% in Cleveland.

On 1986 figures 63,570 people were remanded in custody pending trial. The outcome of 11,466 of these cases is not available, but the remaining cases show that 40% of those remanded in custody were later released without a prison sentence.

If the numbers of remand prisoners are increasing, the conditions for remand prisoners are some of the worst in the prison system, and deteriorating. At Risley Remand Centre in Warrington there have been seven suicides in the last twelve months. The Chief Inspector of Prisons, Judge Stephen Tumin, has said that inmates live in 'barbarous and squalid circumstances'. The remand centre, known to its inhabitants as 'Grisly Risley', is not a decaying Victorian Institution. It was built in 1965 as a showpiece for penal reform.

Other remand prisoners are forced to stay in the confines of police cells where facilities for exercise and recreation are often limited. Many cells are underground. A London coroner, at the inquest on a prisoner who committed suicide after spending 21 days in police cells, described the conditions as barbaric. Facilities for visiting are poor. Prisoners are often moved to a different town at short notice, making it difficult for families and lawyers to visit. Lawyers often find that the facilities for private interviews are non-existent. According to the National Association for the Care and Resettlement of Offenders (NACRO) the number held in police cells each night rose more than four-fold between 1986 and 1987 and tripled to 1,575 by August 1988. In December 1987 51 of the prisoners held in police custody were awaiting psychiatric or medical reports.

In December 1988 six organisations involved in the criminal justice system urged the Home Secretary to resolve the problem of remands in police cells. The Law Society, the Criminal Bar Association, the Crown Prosecution Service, the Association of Chief Officers of Probation, the Justices' Clerks Society, and the London Criminal Courts Solicitors Association described the problem as 'teetering daily on the edge of crisis'.

In March 1988 the Government made things worse by removing an unconvicted prisoner's right (created in 1952) to receive food parcels from outside prison. In a case taken by NCCL the High Court refused to declare the new regulation unlawful.

Private prisons　The Government may, in the circumstances, be more than happy to put out parts of the prison service to private tender. In a Green Paper on private sector involvement in the remand system, the Government has set out options for contracting out the custody of prisoners or services such as providing escorts to and from courts.

But prison reform groups argue that privatisation would be a giant step backwards. Profit would be put before the proper provision of facilities and supervision. Private control would not lend itself to much-needed reforms in the criminal justice system because private firms would have a vested interest in enlarging the prison population. The private sector is not the solution to the appalling conditions in local prisons and remand centres. The Prison Governors Association has called for 'the arm of justice' to remain within the state.

Prisoners' grievances and discipline   In view of the repeated outbreaks of unrest in prisons, including riots and the taking of hostages, it is regrettable that the Government has completely ignored the opportunity (in the Criminal Justice Act 1988) to reform the prison grievance and disciplinary systems. Reforms had been recommended to the Government by the Prior Committee on the Prison Disciplinary System in 1985 and promised in the White Paper which preceded the Act.

The Prior Committee's central recommendation was that responsibility for hearing serious disciplinary charges should be transferred from Boards of Visitors to a new Prison Disciplinary Tribunal with a legally qualified chairman. This would free the Boards to continue their independent role as 'friend' of the prisoner. Prior also recommended a new and much overdue disciplinary code, a reduction in the maximum penalty to 120 days' loss of remission, a range of procedural changes and the availability to those conducting adjudications of legal and procedural advice. All these recommendations remain unimplemented.

8

Intolerance, Discrimination
and Inequality

Race

Racial intolerance is exhibited in prejudice, abuse, racial hatred and
discrimination. Racial disadvantage is a pervasive and deep-rooted
phenomenon, experienced by successive generations, as the House
of Commons Home Affairs Committee reported after its visit to
Liverpool just before the 1981 riots.

Employment   The overall position of black people in the labour
market has worsened in the last ten years. Commission for Racial
Equality (CRE) statistics show that the unemployment rate of black
people has risen to twice that of whites. In many inner city areas the
rate is far higher, even 60-70% in some London boroughs.

In 1984 the Policy Studies Institute concluded that the British job
market had changed little in its hostility to black workers, except to
exclude more of them from work altogether. Based on a nationwide
survey, it found that both Asians and West Indians were found in
jobs that are lower down the occupational ladder than whites.
Continuing racial discrimination at the point of recruitment, it
concluded, was an important factor in maintaining the status quo.

The CRE reported in 1987 that most employers had taken no
action to implement a Code of Practice, introduced in April 1984 to
provide equal employment opportunities for black people. Many
employers were ignorant of the Code's existence. Of those who had
adopted the Code many were found to have a long way to go in
translating policies into action.

The CRE is also deeply concerned at the mounting evidence of
outright racial discrimination in recruitment and selection of young
black people. The 1986 Labour Force Survey (for 1984-1986)
showed that the unemployment rate among black people in the
16-24 age group was 32% compared with 17% for white, with the
rate for Pakistanis and Bangladeshis soaring to 43%.

Ethnic minorities are under-represented in all the professions. In

1987 the CRE reported its concern that in some areas, such as teaching, where the number of black teachers currently training is worryingly low, there is little or no prospect of improvement in the near future. Government funded reseach in 1988 shows that Afro-Caribbean and Asian nurses are becoming 'an endangered species' in the health service because of discrimination in recruitment, deployment and promotion.

In 1985 the CRE informed the Government of the urgent need for specific reforms and amendments to the Race Relations Act 1976: 'The need for legislation that works – and is seen to work – effectively and justly is now critical.' The CRE recommended the expansion of formal investigations but with simplified procedures, greater support for individual complaints through tribunals and courts, altering the definition of indirect discrimination to make it less easy to 'justify' certain practices, the extension of the CRE's powers to issue Codes of Practice, and more effective monitoring of equal opportunities policies. None of these recommendations has been implemented by the Government.

Other areas of discrimination   In May 1983 the CRE served a non-discrimination notice on the London Borough of Hackney following a comprehensive investigation into the allocation of council housing to different racial groups. The CRE found that black applicants and tenants frequently received poorer quality accommodation than whites. For example, blacks were less likely to be given houses and maisonettes and more likely to receive flats. In September 1988 the London Borough of Tower Hamlets was found guilty of discrimination against Bangladeshis in the way it allocated housing.

In July 1988 a firm of estate agents was found guilty by the CRE of discriminating against Asian clients on the basis of 'crude stereotyping'. In a formal investigation the CRE found that a computer programme, which was used to select students for a leading medical school, discriminated against female and black applicants.

These are just a few examples of racial discrimination. The CRE is deeply worried that Britain could face more inner city riots unless the living standards of black people are improved. Discrimination and harassment remain widespread and deep-rooted. In another study the Runnymede Trust says that black workers are no better off today than they were before the Race Relations Act became law twenty years ago.

Meanwhile the Social Research Council reported in 1987 that the 'overwhelming majority' of modern white youth is overtly racist, as well as being politically illiterate and, if unemployed, fundamentally disaffected with society. The study showed that young whites blame society's problems on black people.

Criminal justice system   There is deep prejudice in the police service, particularly against young black men. The misuse of stop and search powers is a common grievance amongst black youth. As we have seen in Chapter 6, the 1981 Brixton disorder was found by Lord Scarman to be in part a reaction to police behaviour. In the USA the Kerner Commission on civil disorder found that police behaviour was the most frequently perceived source of grievance in the black community.

There is evidence to suggest that a disproportionate number of young black males are stopped by the police and that black juveniles are less likely to be cautioned and more likely to be prosecuted than comparable white juveniles. In a Home Office Research Unit study it was found that officers from two London police stations stopped young black males aged 16 to 24 roughly ten times more often than the average. The Policy Studies Institute survey commissioned by the Metropolitan Police in 1983 found that among men aged 15 to 24 the proportion stopped was 63% for West Indians, 44% for whites and 18% for Asians. Only about one in twelve stops led to the detection of an offence. Black people accounted for 17% of those arrested, but for only 5% of the population of London.

In 1988 Staffordshire Police were found guilty of encouraging racial discrimination. They had published a neighbourhood watch bulletin advising householders to note the registration numbers of cars driven by black people. Nationally, there are no members of the ethnic minorities among the senior police ranks of chief constable, chief superintendent or superintendent. Recruitment in the lower ranks has been less than successful. In 1987 only 0.9% of the police force came from an ethnic minority. One black police officer in Yorkshire resigned from the force claiming a racist campaign had driven him out of the force. He alleged he had been called 'Toby' on one course and 'black bastard' on another. In November 1988 a former community policeman in Toxteth told Liverpool Crown Court that he had heard police colleagues racially abusing black people: 'It is pretty rife. You have to be pretty naive not to know that.'

Black people are not only under-represented in the police force. Only 1.9% of the probation service and 0.6% of the prison service come from an ethnic minority. As at January 1987 1.9% of magistrates were from an ethnic minority, although in 1986 the figure of magistrates appointed was 4.5% (compared with 1.7% in 1980).

Studies also show that a disproportionately high number of black defendants are refused bail and remanded in custody. Home Office figures show that a higher proportion of black defendants remanded in custody are subsequently acquitted.

In Birmingham a study in 1979 found that defendants of West Indian background were nearly twice as likely to be committed to the Crown Court as white offenders. A study by the National Association for the Care and Resettlement of Offenders found that black people who offend are twice as likely to go to prison than white comparables, even though they have fewer previous convictions. A disproportionate 14% of prisoners in England and Wales are from the ethnic minorities. This is more than twice the percentage in the general population. A study of juvenile sentencing in Hackney in London between 1984 and 1986 found that black offenders were more frequently sentenced to custody than white offenders. Another study of sentencing of juveniles in North London found that 53% of black youths given custodial sentences had substantially fewer previous convictions than the 33% of white youths.

These figures do not show that black people are more likely to commit crime than white people. They show that there is a marked element of institutionalised racism in the criminal justice system. Regrettably, that racism is shown in the attitudes of the officials of the system.

In an unpublished report for the Home Office the Oxford Centre for Criminological Research claims that racism is an intrinsic part of the prison service. The report is an indictment of prison officers' racist attitudes and systematic discrimination against black people. One prison officer said that he had fought in the war to prevent Britain becoming a German colony only to find it 'infested with West Indians'.

In February 1988 John Alexander, a black prisoner, was awarded compensation for racial discrimination suffered in prison. A prison officer's assessment had described him in this way: 'He displays the usual traits associated with people of his ethnic background, being arrogant, suspicious of staff, anti-authority, devious and possessing a very large chip on his shoulder.'

The judge's nominal award of £50 for damages for 'injury to feelings' was increased by the Court of Appeal to £500. The following month the Court of Appeal awarded £3,000 to Dr Noone, a microbiologist, for 'severe injury to her feelings'. A regional health authority had discriminated against her on grounds of race in turning down her application for a consultancy. Despite her superior qualifications, experience and publications, the interview procedure was described by the tribunal hearing the case as 'little more than a sham'.

As a result of the Alexander case, the Home Office was forced to give 'advice' in November 1988 to prison governors on the need to avoid racially offensive remarks and derogatory language in written reports on individual inmates.

Racial hatred offences   The only positive step taken by the Government to deal with a serious problem is the creation of new racial hatred offences in the Public Order Act 1986. The Act creates six new offences of racial hatred, combining two tests of 'intent to stir up racial hatred' and 'the likelihood of racial hatred being stirred up'. But there are serious weaknesses in the new offences which means that few charges will be brought. The Attorney General must give his consent to a prosecution. Successive Attorneys General have, however, publicly expressed their reluctance to prosecute. They say that unsuccessful prosecutions do more harm than good to racial equality.

Immigration

There is nothing new about racism in the immigration laws and procedures. This country has for many years pursued racially discriminatory policies: in defining those subject to immigration control and the eligibility for admission so as to favour white entrants and in a wide range of discretionary administrative powers which in practice discriminate against black entrants.

In 1968 the Labour Government admitted that the Commonwealth Immigrants Act was racially motivated (to keep out East African Asians). The European Commission of Human Rights provided confirmation in the East African cases that the 1971 Immigration Act and the 1973 Rules provided a system of immigration control which was racially discriminatory.

Other discriminatory measures followed. A rule was created which allowed only British women who were born in the UK to have their husbands or fiances admitted to live with them. Two separate definitions of the family were found, one for EEC workers, the other for the rest of us, with the stringent and discriminatory test of birthplace which keeps out non-British relatives of British people. Immigration officers were reminded in secret instructions to be suspicious of the would-be entrant 'because he belongs to a class of immigrant which has strong economic or other incentives to obtain entry to this country and because of the frequency with which other immigrants of that class have evaded or have attempted to evade immigration controls'.

By 1979, the Government's own statistics proved that refusal of admission by birthplace was discriminatory. Long entry clearance queues developed in the Indian subcontinent despite official assurances to the contrary. But some of the worst treatment of black people was given on entry to the UK. Powers of search of baggage, retention of documents, medical inspection (including internal vaginal examination to determine virginity), detention without the opportunity to apply for bail, and removal from the country without prior right of appeal were just a few of the powers which have been carried out by immigration officers with almost unlimited discretion. These powers continue to exceed considerably the powers of the police. Meanwhile the Home Secretary has unlimited powers to deport when he deems it 'conducive to the public good'.

Within this legal framework and with this 'tradition' of hostility to black immigration, the last ten years has seen fresh acts of institutionalised discrimination. The British Nationality Act 1981 consolidated discrimination in earlier Acts by reclassifying some (mostly black) citizens as British overseas citizens with no rights of entry to the UK. Many black people who entered Britain years ago as British citizens lost their right to be British (the Home Office now has a discretion), because they did not register with the Home Office before the end of 1987 at a cost of £60. The 1981 Act also ended the *ius soli* rule which gave British citizenship to anyone born here.

Since 1983 those seeking entry through marriage have been required to satisfy the much criticised 'primary purpose test'. This test has reversed the burden of proof by requiring evidence from the entrant that the marriage was not only not a marriage of convenience but was also not entered into with the main intention of gaining entry to Britain. With the difficulty of having to prove two negatives, 50% of Asian husbands applying for entry to join their wives have been refused entry under this rule. The rule has no impact on white husbands who seek entry.

In 1984 the Commission for Racial Equality produced a report expressing concern about discrimination in the immigration service.

In October 1988 the Home Office issued a departmental circular warning immigration officers that they could be subjected to disciplinary action if they displayed racial prejudice. But the Home Office made it clear that the new policy was not intended as a criticism of past behaviour; the Government was proud of the immigration service's record.

In 1986 and 1987 the Government clamped down on asylum seekers. It increased long term detention for refugees. Some detainees have been kept locked up often for a year or more. The Government restricted the right to make representations through MPs and agencies for a reconsideration of the Home Office refusal to permit entry. It also continued to restrict a refugee's right to appeal against refusal of entry, by not allowing appeals until after the refugee had been removed from the country. Solicitors acting for refugees were forced to get injunctions against the Home Office to prevent removal. So inadequate were the interview procedures and so poorly carried out, that the High Court intervened time and time again on the side of the refugees.

The problems of refugees have been highlighted in a number of well-publicised incidents. Within days of the Zeebrugge disaster the Government set up the 'Earl William' car ferry as a prison ship off Harwich. Six months later the ship was abandoned and the prisoners bailed; the storm of October 1987 ran the ship aground. In February 1987 the Government tried to put 64 Tamils on a flight to Sri Lanka, but they protested by taking off their clothes on the tarmac at Heathrow.

The intransigence of the Government's policy on asylum-seekers was made clear in the Home Office statement of October 1987 that its officials were 'better placed to assess the likelihood of persecution' than those claiming refugee status. In November 1987 a group of churchmen, politicians and academics formed Charter '87 to press the Government to soften its line on refugees. Churches and temples have also offered sanctuary to those threatened with deportation.

New restrictions in 1987 on the liability of carriers meant that airlines could be fined up to £1,000 for each passenger who entered the UK without authentic documents. In 1988 it became lawful for airlines to hire immigration officers to vet passengers before they boarded their aircraft.

Finally, the Immigration Act 1988 completed the cycle of racism. It removed yet another category from the list of those promised in 1971 that they would be entitled unconditionally to bring their wives and children to live with them in the UK: Commonwealth Citizens who were settled in Britain in 1971. They now have to satisfy immigration officers that they qualify for entry by passing a number of specific tests. The 1971 rule was found by the European Court to be discriminatory against women. It gave rights to husbands to bring in wives, but not vice-versa. Instead of changing the rule to allow wives to bring in husbands, the Government has taken away the rights of husbands unless they can satisfy immigration officers that they can pass the tests about their marriage.

And the 1988 Act goes further. Its provisions include the abolition of rights of appeal against deportation for people who have been here for less than seven years. It strengthens the criminal law against overstayers. It reduces the length of time visitors may stay. It also restricts the important right of MPs to intervene to prevent summary removal from the country. The Government-funded United Kingdom Immigrants Advisory Service described the Act as 'a further curtailment of existing rights which will undoubtedly affect many of our clients adversely'.

Women

Sex discrimination 'If the Good Lord had intended us to have equal rights and to go out to work and behave equally he really wouldn't have created man and woman.' The words of Patrick Jenkin, Secretary of State for Social Services, in 1979 ushered in a decade wanting in Government commitment to women's equality and freedom from discrimination.

The 1975 Sex Discrimination Act had aimed to ensure that women received no less favourable treatment than men in employment, education and the provision of goods and services. But it was far from adequate in the extent of its provisions, particularly in that it did not cover social security, taxation or provision for retirement and pensionable age. It did not provide for legal aid except in that the Equal Opportunities Commission can provide selective assistance and representation. As there was no provision for actions on behalf of a class or group of women, individual women have had to bear the strain of taking cases. As a result few cases have been taken and their success rate, from the beginning, has been very low.

Since 1975 there has been little commitment by any government to implement the spirit, let alone the letter of the Act. What little progress there has been has been forced upon the Government by cases taken to the European court.

Equal pay   In 1982 the Government was found guilty of failing to comply with its obligations under the Treaty of Rome because it had failed to make provision for women to claim equal pay for work of equal value. It had also failed to provide redress for women who wished to challenge their job evaluation schemes if they contained hidden or indirect discrimination. As a result, the Government amended the Equal Pay regulations in 1983. Irene Pickstone, a warehouse employee with a mail order firm, spent four years fighting in the courts for the right to bring a claim at an industrial tribunal for equal pay for work of equal value.

When the Equal Pay Act came into force in 1975 there was some increase in women's pay but since 1981 their pay has remained at just under 75% of men's.

Low pay   Between 1979 and 1988 the number of workers earning below the minimum level recommended by the Council of Europe in its Social Charter increased from 8 to 9.4 million. Nearly six million of this latter figure are women. Government action has eroded protection for low paid workers. In 1980 Section 11 of the Employment Protection Act was repealed. It had allowed workers to claim the 'going rate' for the job. In 1983 the Fair Wages Resolution was removed from government contracts. In 1986 young workers were denied the protection of Wages Councils which set minimum pay levels and other terms and conditions. Women make up 75% of the workers covered by Wages Councils.

In the Local Government Act 1988 the Government ensured that local authorities do not intervene in support of the low waged. It removed the right of local government to practice contract compliance, to enter into contracts only with firms who comply with certain conditions such as promoting equal opportunities and ensuring fair wages. Some local authorities had been in the forefront of promoting positive action to improve women's wages levels and to remove direct and indirect discriminatory practices.

Retirement   Helen Marshall wanted to work until the age of 65, like men. But she had to go to Europe to prove her point. In winning her case she forced the Government to pass the Sex Discrimination Act 1986 which made it unlawful to dismiss women at 60 in the public sector.

The Government used the occasion to repeal legislation concerned with protecting women from working certain hours and at night.

However, this Act did bring partnerships, private households and small undertakings within the ambit of the sex discrimination legislation.

Maternity rights   Successive Governments have weakened the maternity rights of women at work. In 1979 the qualifying period of continuous work with one employer was six months. By 1988 it was two years. The 1980 Employment Protection Act did provide for the first time the right to time off work for ante-natal treatment. But it also took away two rights: the right of women to return after maternity leave to the job they had left, and the right of women to return to work for the same employer where the employer had less than six employees and it was not 'reasonably practicable' to re-employ her.

Carers   13% of women are carers for sick or dependent relatives. But women who have to care for children or elderly relatives have been left without the necessary extra resources, despite the conclusion of the Griffiths Report that responsibility for community care should be placed with local authorities. It is estimated that unpaid carers save the Government up to £5 billion per year. Yet the United Kingdom Government has the lowest levels of statutory nursery provision for the under fives in the whole of the EEC. In 1980 the Education Act removed the responsibility of local authorities to provide nursery care for children aged three to five. In 1985 the Inland Revenue decided to tax employers who paid subsidies to workers for workplace nursery places. In 1985 child benefit was cut by 5%. In 1987 and 1988 it was frozen.

Taxation   In taxation a woman's earnings are still treated as her husband's. In 1988 the Government announced that women would be given independence in the taxation system: the married man's allowance would be abolished and replaced by the married couple's allowance. This allowance will be payable in the first instance to the husband. The poll tax may place additional burdens on women in providing for joint and several liability for couples (see Chapter 4 above).

Social security   In the payment of social security benefits the law discriminates against women. Although the Social Security Act 1980 permitted women to claim for the first time, if they could establish that they were the claiming partner, the Act did not permit women to draw either the Non-Contributory Invalidity Pension or the Invalid Care Allowance. Jacqueline Drake had to take yet another case to Europe to establish the right to receive the latter benefit for the care of her severely disabled mother for whom she had given up work. Anticipating another defeat in Europe the Government allowed women to draw the former benefit, but called it Severe Disablement Allowance and narrowed its scope. Estimates suggest that only 20,000 of the 240,000 women who would formerly have been eligible may now draw this new benefit.

Other measures on social security have been restrictive. The Social Security Act 1986 abolished the universal maternity grant and single payments for maternity items to women on Income Support. It abolished Widows Allowance and raised the qualifying age by which widows could receive full pension rights. 94,000 women lost their right to Maternity Allowance, as a new system of Statutory Maternity Pay was introduced. The rights of parents on Income Support to deduct child care expenses from the amount of earnings to be disregarded for Income Support purposes was removed. Women in low waged families lost out through the withdrawal of free milk and vitamins and free school meals.

Trade unions and employment

In the last ten years successive governments have attacked and undermined important trade union rights. The intolerance of the state to organised opposition has all too readily been directed at trade unions. At GCHQ (see below) the Government has sacked workers for belonging to a trade union. The Public Order Act 1986 severely inhibits picketing. There have been four major statutes since 1979 which have taken away trade union and employment rights: the Employment Act 1980, the Employment Act 1982, the Trade Union Act 1984 and the Employment Act 1988. Yet another Employment Bill was published in December 1988.

The ostensible approach has been to bring militant trade union leaders to heel and give individual trade unionists greater rights within their union. In practice, the Government has sought to impose a rigid form of democracy on trade unions, overriding their existing procedures. At the same time the Government has cut the rights of employees, who therefore need the trade unions in defence of their rights all the more.

The first steps taken by the Government reduced the employment rights of workers to claim that they had been unfairly dismissed. In 1979 the length of service requirement before workers could claim unfair dismissal was extended from six months to one year. In 1980 it was extended to two years for those working for small firms and in 1985 the two-year period was extended to all employers. The burden of proof was then shifted from the employer to the employee in unfair dismissal cases, and the minimum basic compensation award of two weeks' pay was abolished. An employee may now prove a case of unfair dismissal and get nothing. Under the Government's latest proposals, an employee may have to put down a deposit of £150 before the case is heard.

Other changes in the law have enabled employers to evade job protection laws by offering fixed term contracts, reduced guarantee pay for workers, undermined maternity rights, reduced the powers of Wages Councils to set minimum rates for low-paid workers, removed minimum wage protection for young people under 21 altogether, and repealed legislation on undercutting wages. The latest Employment Bill proposes the removal of restrictions on the hours worked by young people and women, and a White Paper published in December 1988 suggests that Wages Councils should be abolished altogether.

The main onslaught on trade unionists came in measures reducing their rights to take industrial action. They include the banning of most forms of secondary action, restricting the right to picket to a striker's own place of work, and the narrow redefinition of 'trade disputes'. These measures infringe the right to strike, the right to organise and the right of freedom of association. They prevent general support for dismissed workers at GCHQ. They make it unlawful for most workers to take action in support of the nurses. They forbid bans on South African produce. They stop attempts to improve conditions in a sweatshop by refusing to handle the company's products. The scope of the secret ballot provisions is so wide that spontaneous walkouts over a sacking or a health and safety problem are made unlawful. The recent draft Code of Practice puts up a whole series of new barriers to effective, lawful industrial action.

The consequences for trade unions are spelt out in penalties. The 1982 Employment Act makes unions liable in damages for the first time since 1906. In the printers', miners' and seafarers' disputes there has been confiscation of property, sequestration and receivership.

Trade unions have always chosen their leaders. Some are elected by the members, others are appointed by an elected executive committee. Each union has elected its leader in the way suited to its particular circumstances and traditions. But the Government, which is the least democratic of all the major political parties in the constitution of its membership (all ministers have been appointed by one person since 1979), has interfered in the traditional running of the unions by imposing precise and costly election provisions.

This and other acts of interference in internal union democracy amount to a denial of freedom of association unparalleled in Western Europe. The Government has reduced individual rights, restricted the collective rights of unions and meddled with union rule books. These are changes in the law which are overtly political. In some cases they appear to be motivated by a desire for revenge for the miners' strike. They have the ultimate effect of accruing more power to central government at the expense of basic freedoms.

GCHQ

In October 1988 the Government finally carried out its threat to dismiss workers at GCHQ, the Government's communications headquarters and intelligence-gathering centre at Cheltenham, for belonging to a union. It is the first time in this country that Government employees have been sacked for belonging to a trade union.

In January 1984 the Government brought an end to the right of GCHQ workers to organise in a trade union. Compensation payments were made to those willing to renounce their union membership. The last 18 trade union officials who had persistently defied the Government by refusing to give up their union rights were threatened with dismissal by way of compulsory retirement after a final warning and last ditch offer of compensation. Ten of the last eighteen were dismissed and the remainder have either been transferred, are considering transfers or have retired.

Behind this struggle lies the Government's claim that membership of a union and the possibility of strike action constitute a threat to the efficient operations at GCHQ and hence a threat to national security. The Civil Servants unions publicly and indignantly reacted to the inference that their members were 'traitors'. The trade unionists argue that the Government's position has been dictated by paranoia over secrecy and hatred of unions. Their offers to enter a no strike agreement had been rejected. The end result has been to deprive workers of a basic right to organise.

Brian Johnson, a loyal Crown employee at GCHQ for 32 years,

did not feel strongly about the union when he first started work at GCHQ: 'But the management encouraged membership and there was never any suggestion that being a union member meant being a rebel. Then in 1984, out of the blue came the ban. I could not believe it. I felt numb. I thought that this could not be happening in England.'

Mike Grindley, chairman of the GCHQ trade unionists and a Mandarin Chinese expert, was fined £500 in a disciplinary hearing for contributing without permission to the BBC radio programme *My Country Right or Wrong*. In a contribution lasting four short sentences he commented sceptically on the system of random exit searches at GCHQ, an aspect of security at GCHQ which had earlier been discussed publicly by the Security Commission (in the wake of Geoffrey Prime's conviction and 32 year sentence for spying in 1982). The producers of the programme used his contribution to show how discreet all GCHQ employees are. Grindley argued in his own defence in the disciplinary hearing that the Civil Service code states that union representatives are free to comment on matters which directly affect their conditions of service. Since then the Government has added to GCHQ's internal code the familiar claim that GCHQ officials are bound by an absolute, lifelong duty of confidentiality.

The International Labour Organisation has condemned the British Government for continuing the ban on trade union membership at GCHQ. The final decision to dismiss employees has been met with walkouts and threatened strikes by civil servants and other trade unionists. Neil Kinnock, the Labour Party leader, described the dismissals as 'an unjustified and undemocratic attack on individual civil liberties'.

In a separate case Sir Peter Marychurch, the Director of GCHQ, withdrew the security clearance of Andrew Hodges, a 22 year old data processor, who told management that he was gay. The Security Commission had recommended that homosexuality should not be an absolute bar in the civil service. In the High Court the judges paid tribute to the courage and integrity of Hodges but decided that Marychurch had a total discretion. They dismissed his appeal.

Travellers

Despite the fact that a nomadic lifestyle is perfectly legitimate, travellers are regularly denied the right to peaceful freedom of movement and assembly and a place to stay. Steps taken by the

Government and the police to curb the rights of this significant minority and the failure to protect the legitimate interests of travellers have exemplified an unacceptable level of state intolerance.

For travellers, the real practical problem is the lack of proper sites. Although the Caravan Sites Act 1968 decreed that every local authority has a duty to provide sites with adequate accommodation, the failure to do so has been widespread. The Government has powers to make local authorities provide sites, but it does not like to use them. Travellers are not a popular political cause. This means that travellers have been forced to use illegal sites and risk facing prosecution.

Some of the worst abuses against travellers came with the growth in the numbers of 'new age' travellers moving towards Stonehenge in 1985 and 1986 at the time of the summer solstice. The Home Secretary described the members of the 'convoy' as 'medieval brigands'. The Prime Minister said she was determined to 'make life difficult for such things as hippy convoys'. Senior police officers described them as 'pollution', talked of strategies to 'neutralise' them, carried out dawn raids and set up road blocks. All the panoply of the state was mobilised, against a small group of people who had adopted an alternative lifestyle.

The Public Order Act 1986 was amended to add a new offence of criminal trespass, despite the general belief that the civil law of trespass and existing police powers were more than adequate, and amid fears that the new law would cause more problems than it would solve. Farmers complain that the police use the new powers inconsistently and with an over-narrow interpretation. The police claim that the extent of their powers is unclear.

The police used powers of dubious legality to carry out a number of operations near Stonehenge. They set up road blocks. They used powers which had been 'developed' in the miners' strike to stop vehicles and turn them away (known as the 'intercept policy'). They created an exclusion zone of five miles around Stonehenge. They closed off roads (misusing the Road Traffic Regulation Act 1984). They stopped travellers and asked a wide range of questions (beyond their powers in the Road Traffic Act 1972), as part of an intelligence-gathering exercise. They obtained an order from the Salisbury District Council banning 'hippies' from the city centre for two specified days to prevent a protest march from taking place.

The police charged large numbers of travellers with serious criminal offences such as unlawful assembly. The gravity of the charges permitted the courts to impose heavy bail conditions, including the requirement 'to leave the county of Wiltshire by midnight'. The serious charges were later dropped or reduced to minor ones. In some cases the police insisted on dragging large numbers of defendants through a crowded market place in handcuffs.

Travellers who were trapped in a field – the 'Battle of the Bean Field' – by the police had their vehicles and property damaged by police in riot gear. The Earl of Cardigan who witnessed the scene said: 'I shall never forget the screams of one woman who was holding up her little baby in a bus with smashed windows. She screamed and screamed at them to stop, but five seconds later 50 men with truncheons and shields just boiled into that bus. It was mayhem, no other word for it.' In Operation Daybreak 440 police were used to evict a sleeping encampment at Stoney Cross. Television viewers were later able to see the spectacle of military over-policing.

Meanwhile, the DHSS were employing Big Brother tactics against traveller claimants. A confidential DHSS report had recommended stricter checks than normal against traveller claimants, a national register of 'convoy' claimants, and a restriction on urgent needs payments because their communal lifestyle meant they could borrow from one another.

'Clause 28'

Clause 28 (of the Local Government Bill) has become Section 28 of the Local Government Act 1988. It bans the intentional promotion of homosexuality by local authorities. It is, perhaps, the centrepiece of the Government's state intolerance of minorities.

The Section was intended to put an end to school teachers who allegedly seek openly to 'recruit' children to homosexuality and who do so with the active support of the local education authority. But if that band of teachers is tiny in number, the likely repercussions of Section 28 are much larger. The row over the obscure publication *Jenny Lives with Eric and Martin*, which was found on the closed shelves of the Inner London Education Authority's central library, has developed into a repressive law.

Wording   Section 28 is imprecisely drafted. It is open to wide and varied interpretation. It prohibits a local authority from intentionally promoting homosexuality or publishing material with the intention of promoting homosexuality. It prohibits a local authority from promoting the teaching in any maintained school of the acceptability of homosexuality as a pretended family relationship.

Ironically, when an attempt to introduce a similar clause was made by the Earl of Halsbury in 1987, the Government opposed the clause. It argued that Halsbury's clause was open to 'harmful misinterpretation', because the distinction between proper teaching about homosexuality and advocating homosexuality as a normal form of relationiship could not be 'drawn sufficiently clearly in legislation'.

Restrictions   Theoretically the prohibition on 'promoting homosexuality' covers every activity in which a local authority engages in furtherance of its duties and responsibilities. It may, for example, seriously curb attempts by local authorities to tackle discrimination and to work with people of all ages to increase understanding of lesbians and gay men. It may cut sex education on homosexual issues from the curriculum in schools. The Arts Council has been advised that Section 28 prohibits almost any literary or artistic activity which has an element of homosexuality. Artistic ventures may be forced to look carefully at their programmes in order to avoid censorship by the local authorities which fund them.

Principles   Section 28 breaches the important principle of equality before the law. At a time when the civil liberties of homosexuals are under increased threat of hostility because of AIDS, the attack on homosexuals must be seen as a direct assault upon this principle and on the rights of minorities to seek to advance their own lawful interests through information and education.

Discrimination   Section 28 makes it more respectable to discriminate against homosexuality. It provides a statutory excuse for discriminating against lesbians and gay men. Homosexual teachers in particular may find themselves the subject of witch-hunts. Section 28 strikes at the heart of a free society, open to information, free from censorship, and tolerant of diversity. Section 28 is a pernicious and detrimental measure.

9

Conclusion

This then is the position after ten years, a decade of decline in the condition of civil liberties. The Government has produced almost a state of peacetime emergency. In the name of national security the Government has censored the media and prohibited trade unions. In the name of anti-terrorism the Government has censored the broadcasters, exercised the power of internal exile without trial, and removed the right of silence. In the name of democracy the Government has withdrawn the right to vote and interfered in the internal running of trade unions. In the name of law and order the Government has minimised the right of public protest. In the name of justice the Government has reduced the right of trial by jury and filled the over-crowded prisons.

Something must be done to win back the lost liberties. A fresh approach is needed to protect individual rights from the power of the state. Changes must be made, even constitutional changes, to avoid the constant plundering of civil liberties.

United Kingdom vs Europe: A Losing Battle

The European Convention of Human Rights has been the principal check against a series of the Government's policies. A series of important decisions of the European Court of Human Rights have embarrassed successive governments by finding that they have failed to comply with the fundamental rights and freedoms set out in the European Convention.

Thanks to decisions by the European Court the Government was forced to stop interrogation techniques such as sleep deprivation which had been used in Northern Ireland. Mental patients under compulsory confinement now have more rights and fairer procedures in the review of their confinement. Homosexuality for consenting adults has been legalised in Northern Ireland. Corporal punishment has been abolished in state schools. Prisoners' rights have been extended, for example the right of access to a lawyer. The

91

laws of contempt of court, under which *The Sunday Times* was banned from writing about the effects of the drug thalidomide, have been amended.

In total some 80 UK laws or regulations have been repealed or amended as a result of proceedings under the European Convention. Not all decisions have been so favourable. The Government's ban on trade unions at GCHQ, for example, was upheld. The conviction of the publisher of the Little Red Schoolbook for obscenity was held not to be in breach of the Convention. Isobel Hilton lost her case against MI5 blacklisting (see Chapter 4). But overall, the European Convention has played a positive role in the protection of human rights in the United Kingdom.

The Government was forced by the European Court to change the law of contempt of court after losing its case against Harriet Harman. In 1980 Harman, then NCCL's legal officer, had shown a journalist documents which had been read out in open court in a case about the validity of prison 'control units'. The Government accused her of contempt of court and won, if only by a majority of 3-2 in the House of Lords. Harman accused the Government of interfering with her right to freedom of expression. The parties reached a 'friendly settlement' and the Government agreed to pay £36,320 in legal costs.

The present use of the European Convention   The full title of the Convention is the European Convention for the Protection of Human Rights and Fundamental Freedoms. The Convention was drawn up by the Council of Europe (a body quite separate from the EEC) in 1950 and came into force in 1953. It was ratified by the UK as an international treaty in 1951, and all 21 member states of the Council of Europe are bound by its terms.

The Convention guarantees most (but not all) civil liberties, including the right to life, freedom from torture, freedom from arbitrary arrest, the right to a fair trial, the right to privacy, freedom of religion, and freedom of expression and assembly.

The Convention is not enforceable in the British courts. Complainants must go to Strasbourg for a remedy. Complaints of breaches of the Convention can be brought by either member states or individual complainants (including organisations and groups of people with a common interest). The UK has allowed complaints by individuals since 1966, and it is this class of case which has been so successful against the United Kingdom. Complaints are dealt with first by the European Commission of Human Rights and may later go to either the European Court of Human Rights or the Council of Ministers.

A successful complaint may be resolved by 'friendly settlement', a negotiated agreement between government and individual. Otherwise the Court will give a judgement stating whether the Convention has been violated, ordering 'just satisfaction' (that is, compensation) where appropriate, and legal costs.

Weaknesses in the process   This is not a speedy process. Complaints may take five years or more to be resolved. The procedure may be expensive. Legal aid is available on only a modest basis. There is no right to a hearing in the important early stages when many complaints are ruled inadmissible. Much of the machinery operates in private. There is no emergency procedure for violations of the Convention.

A Bill of Rights?

There is an evident and urgent need for some kind of Bill of Rights to safeguard our civil liberties. The existing unwritten constitution provides little or no protection against restrictive laws passed by Parliament or repressive executive powers. Statutes do not in the main guarantee positive rights and the courts have no framework of principle within which to operate.

Our law has not been shown to be adequate. There are more individual complaints to the European commission by UK citizens than from any other signatory to the Convention, approximately 800 cases a year. More significantly no other country has lost so many cases; about one third of the decisions against governments have been against the UK. The European Convention has been helpful in some of these cases, but the procedure is cumbersome and remote.

Incorporation of the European Convention?

A brand new Bill of Rights is not a realistic objective in the immediate future. The drafting of a new Bill would be so controversial that it would fail through lack of political will, whichever party was in power. By contrast there has been a broad groundswell of support for incorporation of the European Convention into domestic law for some years. It should, however, be noted that an attempt by Sir Edward Gardiner, a Conservative backbencher, to introduce a

Human Rights Bill to incorporate the European Convention into domestic law failed at an early stage in February 1987 for lack of support. The Bill had received the support of the House of Lords, but failed to get a second reading in the Commons by four votes.

Incorporation does, however, have support from the Standing Advisory Commission on Human Rights in Northern Ireland, from a House of Lords Select Committee in 1978, and from a number of senior politicians of all parties. Lord Scarman, a chief promoter of a Bill of Rights for many years, has said: 'A simple way of securing an enacted Bill of Rights would be to incorporate into our law, as other signatories have done, the European Convention. This is something we can do, if we have the will, without raising any constitutional questions.'

There are also glimmers of interest from the judiciary. The most recent convert is Lord Bridge, the senior Law Lord. In one of the *Spycatcher* hearings he explained in his minority judgment that he had not been in favour before. He had had confidence in the capacity of the common law to safeguard the fundamental freedoms essential to a free society including the right to freedom of speech. He had been converted because his confidence had been seriously undermined by the majority decision (upholding the interim injunctions against three newspapers).

Drawbacks to incorporation of the European Convention   The Convention is by no means an ideal document. Its contents could be much improved. The statements of principle are heavily diluted by exceptions and provisos. Article 11, for example, which protects the right to freedom of assembly and the right to freedom of association, contains exceptions which are 'prescribed by law and are necessary in a democratic society in the interests of national security or public safety, for the prevention of disorder or crime, for the protection of health or morals or for the protection of the rights and freedoms of others'. That exception was used to justify the removal of the right to join a trade union at GCHQ.

Judges, on the whole, are conservative and not over-fond of broad statements of principle on the protection of human rights. Their legal training leads them to the particular rather than the general. The Convention could be narrowly or even negatively interpreted. The 1960 Bill of Rights in Canada was a great disappointment. It was a controversial measure which was introduced without overwhelming support. Decisions in the Canadian courts added little to the protection or promotion of civil liberties. Since then Canada has tried to boost its human rights law by passing in 1982 a Charter of Rights and Freedoms.

But we are already half-way to incorporation. We have ratified the Convention and therefore recognise its principles. We trust foreign judges to make important decisions. Sooner or later we shall have to put our own judges to the test. On balance, incorporation would be likely to make a positive contribution to the protection and extension of civil liberties.

The effect of incorporation of the European Convention   The incorporation of the European Convention of Human Rights into the law of the United Kingdom would have two principal legal effects. First, it would entitle an individual complainant to issue proceedings in the domestic courts (rather than going to Strasbourg) for a breach of the Convention. It would also permit a complainant to apply for an injunction at an early stage in the proceedings, a remedy which is not available in Strasbourg.

Secondly, and quite separately, the domestic courts would have to take account of the human rights guaranteed by the Convention in every case in which one or more of those rights were involved. This would involve all the courts, from the magistrates courts to the House of Lords. Cases involving rights and principles are often heard at the lowest level of the court structure. Was the newspaper seller obstructing the highway? Were the police entitled to move the picket on? Were the contents of the poster insulting? In each of these cases, if the Convention were incorporated, the defence would be entitled to argue that the accused was exercising a legally protected right: freedom of expression or freedom of assembly. The court would be obliged to take the provisions of the Convention into account.

In addition to the legal consequences, incorporation would give civil rights a status above politics and provide a set of values which could be taught in schools and respected throughout life. Incorporation would put pressure on the Government of the day, and its civil servants, to have the tenets of the Convention at the forefront of its mind. The preparation of Government proposals, through Green Paper and White Paper, Law Commission and Royal Commission, would have to take account of the fundamental freedoms set out in the Convention. Incorporation would create a climate of principle.

Proposals   First, the European Convention of Human Rights should be incorporated into the law of the United Kingdom. It is the best system available and it is readily available.

Incorporation could be seen as an interim measure, a partial step to the creation of a Bill of Rights which is more suitable to the existing laws of the United Kingdom. It must also be seen as a testing period for the application of human rights principles by the judiciary.

Secondly, and quite independently of incorporation, Parliament should set to work on a programme of legislative and administrative reform in order to provide better protection for civil liberties. It should pass laws which create positive rights, such as a right of privacy, a right of assembly, greater freedom of information, a statutory code of safeguards for suspects, and stronger anti-discrimination laws. Incorporation of the Convention would be no substitute for these measures.

Thirdly, Parliament should retain after incorporation the power to pass legislation which expressly derogates from the Convention. This would permit legislation reversing an unwanted judicial decision. It would keep Parliament sovereign and give it the last word. Incorporation would mean no more than that the Convention will have the status of an Act of Parliament.

Specific Reforms

Some of the specific reforms which are urgently needed for the protection and promotion of civil liberties, in addition to the incorporation of the European Convention of Human Rights into domestic law, are listed below. The issues to which these reforms relate have been raised in the earlier chapters.

Secrets and Information

The Official Secrets Acts of 1911 and 1939 should be repealed. They should be replaced by a Freedom of Information Act and an Act which penalises spying. The latter would restrict criminal sanctions to the communication of properly classified material in the realms of security, defence and foreign affairs, with a view to punishing only the deliberate betrayal of the nation's secrets to a foreign power.

In this context national security would require a narrow interpretation, not to be defined by ministers of the day as and when they see fit, but clearly and simply by Act of Parliament. A public interest defence is a necessary ingredient of any new criminal offence. So too is the defence of prior publication.

The Government should not have the right to censor material

96

which is likely to be published in the press, on television, on the radio or elsewhere in the media. Editors must be trusted to make their own decisions and take the risk of breaching the criminal law. As Lord Griffiths said in the final *Spycatcher* hearing: 'Ultimately . . . if we are to have a free press we have to trust the editors.'

Civil servants should be allowed to appeal to an independent authority when their conscience prevents obedience to instructions which they consider immoral or unlawful.

Former employees of the security services should be permitted to publish their memoirs, subject to security clearance by their former employers and with the right to appeal to an independent tribunal or ombudsman.

Parliament should pass a Freedom of Information Act to increase the supply of government information to the public. It would establish a public right of access to official information, subject to necessary but narrowly drawn exceptions. Even before the Thatcher years, the Royal Commission on the Press observed in 1977: 'The right of access to information which is of legitimate concern to people, parliament and press is too restricted, and this, combined with the general secrecy in which government is conducted, has caused much injustice, some corruption, and many mistakes.'

The proposals of the Government in its Bill on official secrets should be rejected. They are in some respects more restrictive than under the existing law and will endanger the freedom of the press.

The Zircon affair demonstrated that the two roles of the Attorney General – legal guardian of the public interest and political member of the Government – should be more clearly separated and defined. The Special Branch should be governed by narrowly drawn terms of reference set out by Parliament.

The Security Service Bill should be strengthened substantially to provide adequate and effective safeguards against abuse. In particular there must be provision for independent scrutiny of MI5's work and files, for Parliamentary accountability, and for an effecitve remedy for individuals whose rights are infringed.

Privacy and Confidentiality

Parliament must pass a Privacy Act (or enact legislative reforms in specific areas) to protect the invasion of privacy. Legislation is needed to safeguard the individual by law against the collection and use of personal information without consent. It should provide a sanction in damages under the civil law for the individual who suffers distress or financial loss and provide a corresponding sanction in the criminal law for obtaining confidential information by deception (as the Law Commission proposed in 1974). It should give the aggrieved individual a remedy in the civil law for unlawful surveillance and create a criminal offence of surreptitious surveillance by means of bugging devices (as the Younger Committee proposed in 1972). Protection should be provided for the publication of information which is genuinely in the public interest.

Civil service vetting needs to be reformed. If it is to continue it should be brought under Parliamentary control. Applicants for civil service jobs must know which posts are vetted. If an applicant is vetted out of a job, this fact must be revealed and the applicant given a right of appeal.

The collection and use of personal information relating to the poll tax must be restricted. It is not acceptable that personal information, such as the names of those receiving help from the social services, should be transferred without consent. As a minimum requirement an individual should have a right of access to all of his or her files. The transfer of information should be registered under the Data Protection Act and particularly sensitive information should be exempt from transfer.

The Interception of Communications Act should be strengthened. It provides no real safeguards against the abuses of telephone tapping and bugging, whether done by the state or by private individuals. Full control and protection against surveillance, including judicial warrants for any interception, should alternatively be included in a comprehensive Privacy Act.

The Data Protection Act must be amended to give greater protection to the individual against abuses from the collection and storage of computer data. The Act should apply to all manual records. The practice of charging multiple fees for information held by the same organisation should cease. Alternatively, the Data Protection Act should be repealed and the necessary changes and improvements brought within the scope of a comprehensive Privacy Act.

Police Powers and Accountability

The Public Order Act should be repealed. In its place there should be a new Act which codifies all police public order powers, including those currently found amongst a variety of statutes and in the common law. The new Act should include a statutory right of peaceful assembly, including a positive right to demonstrate and picket. It should also create a minimum public disorder test (of actual violence or immediate threat of violence to persons or property), which would be the sole criterion for public order controls. The new Act would also restrict the number and the vagueness of public order offences.

The Prevention of Terrorism Act should be repealed. Violence must be condemned unequivocally, but the Act provides no answer to terrorist violence, which in the long term can only be solved by political means. The PTA is an Act of savage repression and a denial of fundamental rights. It contains powers which, according to Lord Colville's official report, are a severe restriction on civil rights and an embarrassment to the Government abroad. Those suspected of involvement in violence should be subject to the ordinary criminal law.

The Emergency Powers Act in Northern Ireland should also be repealed. The Diplock courts should be abolished and replaced with full jury trials. The wide powers of the EPA are unacceptable in principle and unnecessary in practice, given the wide powers of the ordinary criminal law. The problems in Northern Ireland are essentially political, not law and order, problems. Emergency legislation has now been in force since 1922 and has failed.

The Police and Criminal Evidence Act should be repealed. It should be replaced by an Act of Parliament which sets out the extent of police powers and the rights of suspects in clear, simple and unambiguous language, so that the ordinary citizen may have access to a readily comprehensible document. The new Act should more clearly define and limit police powers of stop and search, and arrest. It should reduce the length of the period of detention under the law (and associated powers). Above all it should establish the rights of suspects in a statutory code of rights which adequately protects the liberty of the subject and will not lead to false confession evidence.

Codification of the criminal law and criminal procedure is necessary (as a report to the Law Commission has recommended). The law at present is scattered far and wide amongst statutes ancient and modern and in the common law. Simplification is required to provide easy access and understanding for the citizen.

There is an urgent need for strengthening the police complaints procedure in order to bring public confidence into the system. In particular a complaint against the police should be investigated by a body independent of the police (as the Police Federation has also recommended).

Parliament should enact a democratically controlled system of police accountability. The tripartite structure of police, Home Secretary and police authorities should be made a reality. Elected police authorities should have genuine powers over policing policies. The Home Secretary should be replaced as the police authority for London by a democratically elected body.

The use of firearms by the police should be governed by statute, not by secret ACPO manuals or by Home Office guidelines.

Criminal Justice

An Act of Parliament should be passed to ensure that all courts, particularly criminal courts, are readily open to the public and the press and that there shall be no unnecessary restriction on reporting all details. The exceptions, for example in hearings about children, should be clearly defined.

Jury trial should not be restricted on grounds of cost or for any other reasons. The right to trial by jury should be increased. In particular the offence of assaulting a police officer in the execution of his duty should be triable in the Crown Court (as recommended by the James Committee in 1975). Jury trial should be restored in Northern Ireland for 'scheduled offences'. The right of peremptory challenge should be restored.

The right of silence should not be abolished or diminished. As Lord Devlin observed: 'I hope the day will never come when the right to silence is denied . . . we afford to everyone suspected and accused of crime, at every stage to the very end, the right so say: "Ask me any questions and I shall answer none – prove your case".'

The *prima facie* rule should be restored as a necessary safeguard in extradition proceedings.

The system of selection, appointment and training of judges should be reviewed. Judges should be appointed from a wider range of people, including younger people, solicitors and academic lawyers.

The criminal appeal system should be reviewed and changed. The Criminal Appeal Act should be amended to provide a new framework for criminal appeals. In addition an independent review body should be set up to consider possible miscarriages of justice, with the power to refer cases back to the Court of Appeal (a proposal made by *Justice* and endorsed by the House of Commons Home

Affairs Select Committee).

The overcrowding in prisons must be remedied. Steps must be taken to bring about shorter average sentences and fewer sentences of imprisonment, particularly for non-violent offenders. The Government must provide more alternatives to prison and give greater support to existing alternatives. The Bail Act should be amended to emphasise the importance of the right to bail, and courts must be encouraged to release more defendants on bail. Prisons should not be privatised. Prisoners' grievance and disciplinary procedures should be revised to follow the Prior Committee's proposals, including the transfer of serious disciplinary charges from the Boards of Visitors to a tribunal with a legally qualified chairman.

Discrimination and Inequality

There is an urgent need to strengthen the Race Relations Act and to make the law clear, workable and effective. As the Commission for Racial Equality pointed out in 1987, the range and persistence of racial discrimination are insupportable in any civilised society. The CRE must be given more resources to mount on a greater scale systematic investigations into the policies and practices of employers. More special programmes are needed to make the principle of positive action more effective. The racial hatred offences in the Public Order Act should not require the Attorney General's consent before prosecution. The police should give greater priority to dealing with racial harassment and attacks.

Immigration laws and procedures should be comprehensively overhauled. New laws should be passed to provide equal and anti-discriminatory treatment for would-be entrants to the United Kingdom. In particular a new Nationality Act would restore the principle of the *ius soli*, the automatic grant of citizenship by birth on United Kingdom territory. It would also confer British citizenship automatically on all existing British Overseas Citizens who do not hold citizenship of any other country, restore life-long entitlement to registration of pre-1973 Commonwealth settlers, and establish a citizen's right to a passport.

The Sex Discrimination and Equal Pay Acts should be replaced by a new statute which takes account of the requirements of European Community law. The new Act should be based on the principle that every person has the right to be treated equally without differentiation on grounds of sex. Equal treatment for women requires co-ordinated policies to deal with discrimination within the labour market and outside it.

The rights of employees must be restored and strengthened, particularly in relation to claims for unfair dismissal and maternity rights, and must give women and part-time workers full and equal rights in the workplace. Trade union legislation should be reviewed and reformed. Trade unionists should have the right to determine their union's form of internal democracy and to take part in peaceful industrial action. Employees at GCHQ should be permitted to join and be active in a trade union, and have their full employment rights restored.

Section 28 of the Local Government Act 1988 should be repealed. Statutory protection against discrimination on the grounds of homosexuality should be introduced.

Travellers should be given proper sites. The Government's powers to require local authorities to provide sites should be exercised to the full. Special arrangements (through discussion with all interested parties) should be made for new age travellers who wish to go to Stonehenge at the time of the summer solstice, in particular with the provision of temporary sites.

National Council for Civil Liberties

Membership or Affiliation

Individual Members

Individual Membership   £12
Two people at the same address   £15
Students, OAPs Claimants   £6
Any two students, OAPs or Claimants at the same address £10

Organisations

Under 100 Members   £17   251-500 Members £30
101-250 Members   £20   501-1000 Members   £40
Over 1000 Members: Details on Application

I/We enclose a cheque/PO for £ .... membership/affiliation
and £ .... donation: total £ ....
I/We* do/do not require a receipt ☐

I/We accept the aims and the constitution of NCCL. I/We* do not/Our
organisation* does not have objectives which are incompatible with those of
the NCCL, nor am I/are we* member(s) or part of any organisation whose
objectives are incompatible with NCCL.
Delete where applicable.

Signature .... Date ....
Name ....
Organisation (if affiliate) ....
Address ....
....
....

Please send me details of direct debit payment   ☐
Please send my/our details to a local NCCL group   ☐

A copy of the constitution is available from NCCL
NCCL, Freepost, 21 Tabard Street, London SE1 68P

National Council for Civil Liberties

Charter of Civil Rights
and Liberties

We are committed to the defence and extension of Civil Liberties in the United Kingdom and to the Rights and Freedoms recognised by International Law. In particular we are pledged to ensure and safeguard these essential rights:

1. to live in freedom and safe from personal harm.
2. to protection from ill-treatment or punishment that is inhuman or degrading.
3. to equality before the law and to freedom from discrimination on such grounds as disability, political or any other opinion, race, religion, sex, or sexual orientation.
4. to protection from arbitrary arrest and unnecessary detention, the right to a fair, speedy and public trial, to be presumed innocent until proved guilty, and to legal advice and representation.
5. to a fair hearing before any authority exercising power over the individual.
6. to freedom of thought, conscience and belief.
7. to freedom of speech and publication.
8. to freedom of peaceful assembly and association.
9. to move freely within one's country of residence and to leave and enter it without hindrance.
10. to privacy and the right of access to official information.